D0387281

Social Scientists and Politics in Canada

SOCIAL SCIENTISTS AND POLITICS IN CANADA

Between Clerisy and Vanguard

STEPHEN BROOKS and ALAIN G. GAGNON

UNIVERSITY LIBRARY

McGill-Queen's University Press
Kingston and Montreal

© McGill-Queen's University Press 1988
ISBN 0-7735-0663-2

Legal deposit second quarter 1988
Bibliothèque nationale du Québec

Printed in Canada on acid-free paper

This book has been published with the help of a grant from the Social Science Federation of Canada, using funds provided by the Social Sciences and Humanities Research Council of Canada.

Canadian Cataloguing in Publication Data

Brooks, Stephen, 1956–
   Includes index.
   Bibliography: p.
   ISBN 0-7735-0663-2
   1. Social scientists–Canada–Social conditions.
   2. Social scientists–Quebec (Province)–Social conditions.
   3. Social sciences and state–Canada–History–20th century. 4. Social sciences and state–Quebec (Province)–History–20th century. 5. Canada–Politics and government–1935–   . 6. Quebec (Province)–Politics and government–1936–1960. 7. Quebec (Province)–Politics and government–1960–   . I. Gagnon, Alain, 1954–
   . II. Title.
   JA76.B76 1988   305.5′52   C88-090167-5

Material in Part One has appeared in modified form in Alain Gagnon, ed. *Intellectuals in Liberal Democracies* (New York: Praeger 1987) and is reprinted by permission of the publisher.

UNIVERSITY LIBRARY
Lethbridge, Alberta
186607

For Christine and Françoise,
who inspired the writing
of this work

Contents

Tables and Figures

TABLES

FIGURES

Acknowledgments

A number of debts were incurred during the research and writing of this monograph. Assistance in the collection of data was provided by Thomas Bird of Statistics Canada, Max von Zur-Meuhlen, and Colin Stewart. Claude Galipeau provided research support at an early stage in our investigation into the political roles of social scientists in Quebec. The general form of this work has benefited from the comments of Kenneth McRae and Jane Jenson, both of Carleton University, at a conference on the role of intellectuals in liberal democracies held in Ottawa in October 1985 as part of a comparative project intended to complement the Canadian perspective of the present study. We would also like to thank the Social Science Federation of Canada for a publication grant under its Aid to Scholarly Publications Program. The comments and suggestions of the three anonymous reviewers were most helpful. We gratefully acknowledge the unflagging encouragement of Philip Cercone, Executive Director at McGill-Queen's University Press, and the care taken by Joan McGilvray, Coordinating Editor at McGill-Queen's, as the manuscript evolved into a book. Finally, we would like to thank the departments of political science at Carleton University and the University of Windsor for secretarial and financial support. Particular mention must be made of Barbara Faria, who amidst numerous competing pressures always found time to type our material, and Lucia Brown, Nancy Gurnett, and Veronica Edwards of the Word Processing Centre at the University of Windsor.

Except where otherwise indicated, we take responsibility for all translations in this book.

Social Scientists and Politics in Canada

Introduction

The relation of the intellectual to politics dates back at least to Plato. Although frustrated in his attempts to have an immediate effect on politics through his instruction of Dion of Syracuse, part of Plato's intellectual legacy is the idea of the philosopher-king and, more generally, the prescriptive notion that political decisions should be entrusted to the wisest members of the community. According to Plato, the capacity to govern wisely and justly requires deliberate application and can be attained by only a few. Thus the well-ordered political system should be capped by a thin stratum of intellectuals who have been educated to their public responsibilities.

In various civilizations throughout recorded history, learned men, scribes, priests, and mandarins have occupied a prominent place in the politics of their society. Unlike the Platonic model of rule by intellectuals, the influence exerted by these groups typically has been through the role of counsellor to the king. Their ability to shape political decisions rested on an acceptance of their claim to possess a body of knowledge, reasoning skills, or powers of divination not shared by other members of society. These groups of intellectuals exercised influence from within the established power structure, constituting what T.S. Eliot referred to as the "clerisy," the intellectual defenders of the status quo.[1] Whether this intimate and supportive relationship to the politically powerful is inconsistent with the vocation of the intellectual is a matter of considerable disagreement.

Two opposing views contend in the literature on the political role of intellectuals. One takes its inspiration from Karl Marx's famous aphorism, "The philosophers have only interpreted the world, in various ways. The point is to change it."[2] The other finds expression in Julien Benda's *La Trahison des clercs*,[3] arguing that the intellectual vocation precludes *engagement*, and that the true role of the intellectual is to stand in opposition to lay opinion and the practical world as the defender of the universal and the

Table 1

Four Interpretations of the Class Position and Political Role of Intellectuals

Interpretation	Political Function	Class Status
Embourgeoisement of the intellectuals, as they increasingly become part of a state-centred, new middle class	Legitimation of the existing system of social and economic power	Petit bourgeois
Proletarianization of the intellectuals, as their objective status becomes less and less distinguishable from other wage labourers	Revolutionary potential, mobilizing subordinate classes	White collar proletarian
The governing-class or ruling-elite theory, most often advanced in the case of developing or revolutionary societies	Leadership in modernizing, societies, and repression in post-revolutionary societies	Class unto themselves
The relatively classless status of intellectuals, where they are capable of detached analysis of politics	Critique, independent of the narrow interests of any group or class	Classless

Source: This table was constructed from the summary in Robert Brym, *Intellectuals and Politics*, (London: George Allen and Unwin 1980) 12–13.

abstract. This distinction is roughly co-extensive with a division between those who view intellectuals as allied to a social class or as constituting a class themselves, and those who view intellectuals as relatively classless. These contending views are summarized in the following adaptation of Robert Brym's survey of the literature on intellectuals and politics.[4]

The first interpretation in table 1 derives from Marxist analysis. Intellectuals are seen as agents of conservatism, who act to reinforce and perpetuate a system of social inequality. This is true not only of those most closely associated with capital, i.e., economists and intellectuals teaching in business schools, but also of those in the social sciences generally. Eric O. Wright refers to the reproductive function of intellectuals–their perpetuation of the ideological hegemony of the dominant class.

This essentially Gramscian understanding considers that the main political function of intellectuals is to support the fundamental values on which the system of capitalist property relations is based.

As producers and disseminators of symbolic goods and intellectual capital—symbolic goods being considered as immediate products and intellectual capital as accumulated knowledge—intellectuals can be considered both in terms of their roles as teachers and researchers, and as experts.[5] While the roles of teacher and researcher can be characterized as *academic* labour (i.e., the production of symbolic goods and intellectual capital, within a given scientific field, for a clientele of colleagues and competitors), the role of expert, according to Turmel, can be characterized as *intellectual* labour (i.e., the "marketing" of symbolic goods and intellectual capital).[6] Thus intellectuals have self-reproducing and legitimizing functions as well as performing a supportive function in the economic and political fields. As teachers and researchers, intellectuals ensure that their intellectual capital is kept sufficiently up-to-date to maintain their social value. As experts, they contribute to the advancement of technology and knowledge as tools of a greater mastery over both nature and society.

The role of teacher, however, is not limited to the self-reproduction of intellectuals as academics or as holders of specialized knowledge. As P. Bourdieu and J.-C. Passeron note, education also performs a social function in reproducing and legitimating the class structure of society, and in maintaining order. This function is performed by means of selection and elimination within the student population, the channelling of students into different disciplines, the evaluation of their work, and the teaching of the "dominant arbitrary culture."[7]

This general ideological function is not necessarily unidirectional. While Bourdieu and Passeron's analysis establishes the relationship between the academic role of intellectuals and their role in social reproduction and legitimation, the role of the academic intellectual as researcher must also be examined. The focus here is on the intellectuals' role as definers of society, inasmuch as intellectuals "give meaning to reality, establish the codes by which it is perceived, the frameworks superimposed on it."[8] It is as researchers (and, to a certain extent, as experts), through the marketing of symbolic goods and intellectual capital, that intellectuals construct definitions of society or, to apply Lamont's terms, "social reality." It is at this level that contradictions may appear between the role of the intellectual and the functions of reproduction and legitimation. These contradictions will be even more important when society is in transition and the class structure is in the process of a major transformation. In such a context the intellectuals' reproductive function can be changed into its opposite, a revolutionary function.

Some intellectuals may provide ideological support for the process of transformation and reorganization of a dominant class (Gramsci's "new intellectuals"), while others may fail to adapt to this process of modernization and thus remain in ideological support of a previous order (Gramsci's "traditional intellectuals"). This open-endedness of the effects of social transition on the function of intellectuals is also related to their class position—to the fact that they are members of the *petite bourgeoisie* and as such find themselves between the "fundamental social groups."[9]

Finally, intellectuals, in their role as experts, perform a distinct administrative function in the economic, political, and intellectual fields. This is related to Antonio Gramsci's definition of intellectuals, particularly organic intellectuals, as the staff of a fundamental social group or class. Thus "intellectuals are the dominant group's 'deputies' exercising the subaltern functions of social hegemony (at the level of civil society) and political government (at the level of political society or the state)."[10] The function of reproduction in the context of the transformation and reorganization of class forces can also be related to the pursuit of self-interest, insofar as these class developments may call for the expansion of administrative positions while at the same time enhancing social value for intellectuals and their roles.

Given the fact that they do not own the means of production, by what reasoning are intellectuals assigned a petit-bourgeois class status? The second interpretation identified in table 1, the proletarianization thesis, argues that since most intellectuals typically lack property, and depend for their livelihoods on the incomes they earn from their association with a large organization, their objective class position, as "intellectual labourers," is reduced to that of the working class. Bettina Aptheker and Alain Touraine contend that the contemporary capitalist economy treats intellectual production, on a par with other forms, as an activity oriented toward the production of exchange commodities.[11] Thus intellectuals both within and outside of academe are workers no less than individuals working in a factory or in a bureaucratic organization. However, this argument fails to acknowledge the important status differences that distinguish intellectuals from other propertyless groups under capitalism. As Brym observes, "What does distinguish [these groups] is the fact that members of the new middle class in general and intellectuals in particular have higher incomes, more prestige and more power than manual workers. In other words, it is not their relationship to the means of *production* which makes intellectuals members of the middle class, but their relationship to the system of *distribution* of social rewards."[12]

In order to bridge the gap between indications of intellectuals' dependent status as a salariat in the employ of institutions integrated into the system of capitalist production, and persistent evidence of their relative autonomy in defining their work and their influence as experts and creators or purveyors of "intellectual capital," it has been argued that intellectuals occupy a "contradictory" class position. From the standpoint of their political involvement the significance of this ambiguous location between labour and capital is twofold. First, it recognizes that intellectuals may be critical of the social order, and therefore is a more realistic conceptualization than the over-deterministic characterization of intellectuals as defenders of the values which underpin capitalist hegemony. Second, the contradictory class position of intellectuals should make them especially sensitive to contradictions in capitalist society. This second argument has been applied in attempts to understand the nationalist analysis that has become increasingly popular among social scientists in Canada since the 1960s.[13]

All Marxist interpretations of the political significance of intellectual activity deny the possibility of the intellectual independent of class ties. In his polemical *Les Chiens de garde* (The Watchdogs), Paul Nizan puts forward an argument that is commonly associated with the French Marxist existentialist Jean-Paul Sartre, and which has become a commonplace of contemporary Marxism. Nizan maintains that intellectual detachment from society (and therefore the classlessness of intellectuals) is not possible. "Abstention is a choice," one that effectively supports the status quo.[14] He thus turns Benda's *trahison* on its head by arguing that the real treason is not political *engagement* but the pretence of impartiality. This view informed popular expression in the student radicalism of the 1960s, embodied in such slogans as "If you're not part of the solution, you're part of the problem." Nizan accuses university professors of complicity with the dominant class by virtue of their general failure to challenge the values that support the social and economic status quo. The fact that he was writing in and with reference to France, where university professors are state functionaries, probably influenced his characterization of the university as the "spiritual lever of the state," performing a role in modern society that once belonged to the church.[15]

Nizan and later Marxists are not blind to the fact that members of the intellectual community, both inside and outside the university, often are critical of the established order – even engaging in forms of political activism such as petitions, demonstrations, public commentary, and party involvement. This criticism and the moderate forms of engagement through which it is expressed are dismissed as inconsequential on the grounds that none of them involves a fundamental negation of the values and institutions that are challenged. Through a nice piece of reasoning, some Marxists suggest that criticism and action requiring no sacrifice of individual comfort or security effectively legitimize the social order by demonstrating the possibility for dissent. This explains why communist intellectuals often have directed their greatest vituperation at social democrats, who might be thought to be comparatively close to them in ideological terms. Briefly put, their argument is that a left-wing movement that operates within the ground rules of liberal democratic institutions and does not insist on the inevitability of social revolution undermines the possibility of fundamental change by purveying the illusion that change can be achieved without demolishing the existing society. What defines one's class allegiance is not what one professes to believe in, but one's action or failure to act. By this reasoning, social democrats are, for practical and class purposes, bourgeois apologists.

The governing-class interpretation of intellectuals in politics, the third interpretation in table 1, is associated with those modernizing and revolutionary societies in which the most educated strata of the population have acquired control of the state apparatus, often through their leadership of the sole political party. It offers little help in understanding the political significance of intellectuals under advanced capitalism. Even in the case of societies in which an intellectual elite appears to have spearheaded the drive for revolution, political independence, or modernization (the Russian Revolution being a major case in point), it may be that the intellectuals' *inherent* power is less than their political prominence suggests. Barrington Moore observes that "intellectuals as such can do little politically unless they attach themselves to a massive form of discontent. The discontented intellectual with his soul searchings has attracted attention wholly out of proportion to his political importance, partly because these searchings leave behind them written records and also because those who write history are themselves intellectuals. It is a particularly misleading trick to deny that a revolution stems from peasant grievances because its leaders happen to be professional men or intellectuals."[16]

Seymour Martin Lipset and Asoke Basu suggest that the power of intellectuals is exercised in a more subtle way than through overlapping membership in the intellectual and ruling classes. Lipset and Basu argue that the intellectual elite, centred in the universities, performs a gatekeeper function in relation to the values that find expression in politics. "More and more [the university] has become the major source of all elites, who must be certified as competent by their passage through the university."[17] Thus, the socialization of individuals who will occupy elite positions in society's various sub-systems affords intellectuals a crucial influence over the dominant ideas that "infiltrate into the summits of most other key institutions."[18] This idealistic conception (not in the colloquial sense of unrealistic, but in contrast to materialistic) appears to be a sociological restatement of Keynes's famous remark that practical men of affairs often are the unwitting slaves of dead economists. Raymond Aron expresses a similar view on the influence of intellectuals when he writes that "the theories taught in universities become, within a few years, truths accepted by ministers or administrators."[19] The question of whether the ideas purveyed by intellectuals are generated within the university relatively independently of material conditions, or whether intellectuals articulate values determined by social and economic forces, is left begging.

The fourth interpretation of the relationship of intellectuals to politics is based on a particular conception of intellectual activity. According to this view, a view more normative than empirical, the proper vocation of the intellectual is critique. To paraphrase Benda, who argues this position in *La trahison des clercs*, the original and proper role of the intellectual is to stand in opposition to lay opinion and the practical world as the defender of the abstract and the universal, and therefore independent of any class. Benda contrasts the disinterestedness of the intellectual *as he ought to be* with the partisan, and especially nationalist, orientation which he saw as characteristic of his contemporaries. "They proclaim that intellectual functions are only respectable to the extent that they are bound up with the pursuit of a concrete advantage, and that the intelligence which takes no interest in its objects is a contemptible activity."[20] However, to the extent that intellectuals are nationalists, the defenders of a particular economic class, or advocates of some other partial interest, their capacity to exercise a moderating influence over the passions of the masses is diminished.

A conception of the intellectual's appropriate vocation similar to Benda's advocacy of apoliticism and social detachment is the ideal of academic professionalism. Especially in North America, the intellectual community has long been identified with the university, an institution that has provided the security for the pursuit of knowledge independent of utilitarian motives and social conventions. According to this view, the university-based intellectuals' attempts to advance knowledge and solve problems within their disciplines has precluded political engagement, for two reasons. First, the quality of research and teaching, as well as the universality of the knowledge generated by intellectuals, would be diminished if the problems they studied and their manner of investigating them were influenced by a desire to be socially relevant or, worse, to advance particular political values. Second, not only the status of the university as a place where knowledge and ideas are valued for their own sake, but also whatever measure of independence from the state and social pressures it enjoys, would be endangered if academics behaved as propagandists and partisans. Of course, the university has always fallen short of this ideal. Knowledge is not a socially disembodied commodity, a fact historically expressed in the response of the Athenian state to Socrates' teaching and the reaction of the church to Galileo's "heresy." Ideas may point to inescapable conclusions which must lead to action, and thus impose an obligation to criticize institutions and values that deny their truth.

Among the factors which Benda argued were responsible for what he saw as a betrayal of the intellectuals' proper function was the positivistic social science which he considered to have supplanted the humanistic tradition of social inquiry based on the learning of Antiquity. Yet the case for positivism rested on its disposition toward, and belief in, the possibility of discovering *universal* laws of human behaviour. Indeed, positivistic social science has given rise to another understanding of intellectuals as independent of class interests: the intellectual as "expert." This view is so widely held in the contemporary social sciences, being embraced most fully in the United States, especially in the discipline of economics, that it may be argued to constitute the dominant conception of the relationship between the social sciences and politics. This conception sees social scientists as the generators of knowledge that can be applied to the improvement of public policy. Kenneth Boulding expresses this view when he writes that "the rise of knowledge of social systems ... has within it the seeds of their control, that is, the development of ideal images of the future within the minds of those who have the power to achieve them."[21] Boulding's treatment of the sociosphere–the realm of human behaviour which is the subject of the social sciences–as analytically similar to physical and biological systems is evident when he writes, "I have argued ... that if we were going to take the social sciences seriously we should at least establish a world network of social data stations, analogous to weather stations. They would take constant measurements and readings of the social system around them by standardized and carefully sampled methods and feed the information into a central processing agency as weather stations collect information about the atmosphere and feed it to weather bureaus."[22]

Virtually by definition, the expert is engaged in a utilitarian activity, bringing specialized knowledge to bear on concrete problems in order to aid in their solution. Presumably, expert knowledge is not by its nature supportive of some social interests rather than others. The charge that intellectuals who sell their skills to organizations that define the object of study for them are legitimizing the established social order is based on two features of such activity. First, there is a vast imbalance between the resources in money and prestige available to disorganized and subordinate groups as compared to organized and socially dominant ones. The state is by far the largest buyer of social science expertise. To the extent that its principal function is the maintenance of social order, the state's interest is in information and analysis that enable it to cope with destabilizing tendencies, not in ideas that are fundamentally critical of the social and economic system over which it presides. Second, experts generally are employed for instrumental purposes: to solve a problem or to provide justification for a course of action, not to determine goals. The opportunities are greatest, of course, for social scientists, and especially economists. Indeed, the dramatic growth of the social sciences in the twentieth century has been largely due to the expansion of the public realm, as the authority of the state has penetrated more and more aspects of individual life and social relationships.

To what extent have social scientists been successful in shaping public policy through their roles as experts? Obviously, the answer varies between different countries, depending on a number of factors: the particular requirements of the economic and social systems; the structure of opportunities for social scientists' participation in the policy-making process; and what has rather encompassingly been called the "policy style" of the political system in question.[23] However, certain cross-national generalizations are possible. First, the development of the welfare state and the increasing recourse by governments to Keynesian economic policies and other forms of intervention in the economy have led to the employment (whether directly, as state employees, or indirectly, as researchers under contract) of large numbers of social scientists—especially economists but also sociologists, psychologists, and political scientists. Writing of the increased importance of technocratic decision-making within the state (including technocrats with social science backgrounds), Lipset and Basu observe: "These trends which greatly benefit intellectualdom as a stratum are seen by some as reducing the historic tension between power and intellect."[24] This is the "end of ideology" thesis, which holds that consensus on the general ends of policy and the accumulation of knowledge about social and economic phenomena have transformed the nature of the political process from conflict over fundamental ends into dispute over the means toward their achievement.

This first generalization suggests a vastly increased field for the participation of social scientists in politics, as experts whose specialized knowledge and skills are essential to problem solving. However, despite the general proliferation of policy analysis functions within the state, and the elaboration of a network of research funding and communication between universities and institutes on the one hand, and the state on the other, there is a general consensus that the rational model of policy-making, in which knowledge and analyses by social scientists constitute the principal determinants of public policy, has not succeeded in displacing modes of policy-making that presuppose conflict.

Thus, a second generalization observes that the actual contribution of social scientists as experts to the resolution of public policy questions is usually minor, or at least oblique. This has led to reassessments of the relationship of social scientists to public policy, and suggestions that their function is properly understood as either *enlightenment* (generating knowledge and analyses which may percolate into the political process)[25] or *legitimation* (lending scientific respectability to a decision arrived at on other grounds).[26] It is evident that either of these functions can be performed without the research interests of the social scientist being linked closely and deliberately to the resolution of a particular social or economic problem. For example, the work of psychologists in the areas of learning theory and cognitive development contributed to the political debate over desegregation in the United States during the 1950s and 1960s through the use made of their findings by various interests. Of course, it is a short step from scientific investigation of phenomena with manifest political significance to *engagement* in support of particular policy reforms. This is suggested by Frank Knopfelmacher when he remarks that intellectuals may wield indirect political influence by activating or articulating oppositional publics.[27]

Obviously the expert function is not limited to intellectuals in the social sciences. However, the relationship of the social sciences to politics is distinguished by two related features. The first is the subject matter studied by social scientists, namely, the range of human behavior and the causes underlying that behavior. The premise of the social-scientific enterprise is the belief that behavior is not random, and that the causal laws underlying social phenomena are ultimately discoverable. Flowing out of the tradition established by Saint-Simon, Comte, and Marx, the social sciences are empirical in methodology, though a wide range of techniques and analytical frameworks is employed in different disciplines and even within the same discipline. But because social scientists are also part of the world of action and motivation that they interpret, questions arise about the relationship of intellectual activity and its products to individual and collective interests.

Therefore, the second feature of the social sciences which renders them of particular political significance is their ideological import. It is not necessary that social scientists be aware that they perform such a function. Indeed, some Marxists argue that for purposes of mystification it may be all the better if social scientists appear to themselves and others as impartial students of society, independent of any class attachment. To better understand this ideological function it is useful to contrast the liberal and Marxist understandings of the relationship of the social sciences to political power.

The central features of the Marxist critical interpretation have been described by Alvin Gouldner in his analysis of what he labels "academic sociology."[28] Gouldner's observations apply to the social sciences in general, though the particular focus of his analysis is the discipline of sociology. Gouldner argues that American sociology, which he sees as epitomized in the work of Talcott Parsons, is voluntaristic ("a stress on the autonomy and *causal potency* of moral values in determining social outcomes")[29] and focused on society's integrative system rather than on conflict and its repression. Critique of the social system occurs within a broad acceptance of the major premises that underlie the socio-economic system, particularly its basic property institutions. The needs of the welfare state for information and personnel have shaped the institutionalization of the social sciences. State funding of research has been a major factor orienting the social sciences toward the sort of problem solving that is congenial to the needs of the welfare state, treating social and economic disorders as problems for which there are solutions that do not require the negation of the values on which liberal capitalist society rests. According to Gouldner, the complicity between social scientists and the state goes further to include a legitimation function whereby social scientists lend their authority as scholars to problems that the state recognizes and is prepared to address. "Once committed to ... intervention the state acquires a vested interest of its own in 'advertising' the social problems for whose solution it seeks financing. In other words, the state requires social researchers that can expose those social problems with which the state is ready to deal."[30]

Can this argument be supported on the strength of the fact that a large proportion of the funding for social science research comes directly, through grants, or indirectly, through salaries, from the state? In fact the problem-solving orientation was evident in the institutional beginnings of American social science well before the advent of heavy state support for scientific research. In their discussion of the origins of scientific planning, Robert Scott and Arnold Shore quote Albion Small, founder of the *American Journal of Sociology*, who in the first issue of that journal wrote, "The work of the discipline was to increase our present intelligence about social utilities ... [to achieve] more effective combination for the general welfare than has thus far been organized."[31] Small's expectations were not unrepresentative. Scott and Shore remark upon the optimism which characterized fledgling sociology and social philosophy in the United States: "Ward, Ross, Small, Dewey, James and Cooley all exude a sense of confidence in the possibility of creating a sociology relevant to the great social challenges of the day. They felt certain that this new science would be equal to the task of ameliorating social evils."[32]

Influenced by the methodological rigour of German social science, American sociology was confident of its role in shaping a better society in the Age of Progress. Traditional methods of historical research and philosophical inquiry increasingly became unfashionable as empirical methodology gained prominence. The "Wisconsin Idea," involving the participation of social scientists in the policy process through consultation and, generally, as sources of expert advice, embodied what Hugh Hawkins has described as the "Ideal of Objectivity."[33] The political implications of this positivistic social science are described by Gouldner: "Insofar as the "positive" implied an emphasis upon the importance of scientifically certified knowledge, it was using social science as a rhetoric, which might provide a basis for certainty of belief and might assemble a consensus in society ... In other words, Positivism assumed that science could overcome ideological variety and diversity of beliefs."[34] Thus, positivist epistemology and contemporary levels of state support for social scientific research together explain the essentially conservative ideological function of the social sciences.

Whereas the Marxist analysis denies the independence of social scientists and views them collectively as adjuncts to the welfare state under advanced capitalism, the liberal understanding argues that it is precisely in capitalist society that the opportunities for a critique of existing institutions and social relations are greatest. Frank Knopfelmacher writes, "Capitalism, wherever it came into being successfully, brought in its wake, or was perhaps even preceded by, a mental climate which favoured rationalism (in Weber's sense)—that is, the habits of systematic application of empirical concepts to human affairs and the type of commerce with nature which was such that beliefs and social practices gradually ceased to be regarded as 'hallowed'."[35]

Following Benda, Knopfelmacher considers the intellectual's proper function to be critique, and argues that alienation is a necessary condition for the effective exercise of this function.[36] The political relevance of intellectual activity resides in the pursuance of critique, whereby their ideas "will have a bearing on prevailing modes of thought and belief concerning social and political issues."[37] This is an idealistic conception of the exchange between ideas and action, according to which the critical views of intellectuals, including social scientists, trickle down into society both through the socialization of political and economic decision-makers and through the mobilization of particular interests around the ideas articulated by intellectuals.

According to the liberal view, social-scientific knowledge can be politically significant in two different ways. The first, as Knopfelmacher suggests, is as critical leaven in a pluralistic market of competing interests. The weight of scientific authority may not be decisive or immediate in determining an issue's outcome, but knowledge about society and interpretive frameworks for understanding it have some independent influence on social behavior. Some examples may illustrate this point. The ideas of the Fabians are credited with contributing to the development of the welfare state in Britain.[38] In Canada the intellectuals who joined the League for Social Reconstruction, and who were influential in shaping the policy platform of the social-democratic Cooperative Commonwealth Federation (CCF), can be argued to have had an indirect role in the development of social reforms that eventually would be instituted by CCF governments in Saskatchewan and by the Liberal government federally.[39] The adoption in Canada of Keynesian fiscal policy, involving the management of aggregate demand and assumption by the state of responsibility for stable levels of employment and economic growth, doubtless would have occurred after World War II under the pressure of the demonstrated effectiveness of Keynesianism in other western countries, and the imperative need for stabilization after the economic chaos of the 1930s. However, the particular timing of this extension of the Canadian state's economic role appears to have been influenced significantly by W.C. Clark, a Cambridge-trained economist who, as deputy minister of finance, in 1945 persuaded Mackenzie King of the necessity of such a course.[40]

The example of Clark suggests the second way in which social-scientific knowledge may have political implications: through the immediate channel of the social scientist as expert. Here there is no question of critical detachment from the social system. Instead, the specialized knowledge of the expert is called on to address some specific problem or constellation of problems, and to recommend steps to be taken, in order to attain ends which are *not* determined by the expert. At the highest level this is the role played by a Kissinger, a Brezinski, or a Schlesinger: the role of counsellor to the king. Of course, the vast majority of expert advice enters the political system at less rarified levels: either through the employment of social scientists within the permanent state apparatus, including such para-public bodies as independent advisory councils and state-funded research institutes, or through such temporary agencies as special committees, royal commissions, task forces, and contracted research. The Marxist tends to see a confirmation of the social sciences' subordination to the needs of the welfare state in this complex network of expert advice operating within a problem-solving framework which lends tacit support to the hegemony of capital. The liberal, however, sees evidence of the social utility of intellectual activity, and opportunities for rationalism in public policy.

Nevertheless, the liberal understanding of the relation of social scientists to politics does not resolve the difficulty of reconciling objectivity and participation. According to Henry Kissinger, "the intellectual as expert is rarely given the opportunity to point out that a query delimits a range of possible solutions or that an issue is posed in irrelevant terms. He is asked to solve problems, not to contribute to the definition of goals."[41] The critical distance of the social scientist from his subject, essential to objectivity, may be lost when expert knowledge is viewed in merely instrumentalist terms. This is a problem only if the practice of critique is considered vital to the intellectual vocation. A possible middle ground between the roles of expert and critic has been suggested by Carol Weiss in her argument that social scientists can perform an enlightenment function, influencing "the way that a society thinks about issues, the facets of the issues that are viewed as susceptible to alteration, and the alternative measures that it considers."[42] This is broadly similar to Lipset's argument, discussed earlier, that the political influence of social scientists is experienced indirectly through their capacity to shape the lenses through which society views itself. In any case, this is a view that attributes to ideas an independent significance which the materialist understanding of Marxist commentators denies.

The interpretations surveyed in the preceding pages can be largely reconciled by the concepts of legitimation and social change. Legitimation involves the process of lending support, through one's words or actions, to established institutions and dominant values. It is not the same as propaganda, nor does it require an outward show of commitment to the status quo. Any society, unless undergoing revolutionary upheaval, will possess a dominant culture whose images and explanations of social reality support an established order. Intellectuals who are comfortable with the established social order will contribute to its maintenance through the creation and dissemination of its images and explanations—a conservative ideological function that they can perform in the lecture hall, through the media, in their writings, through partisan involvement, or in the employ of the state as experts on some area of social behavior. These intellectuals comprise the clerisy, the intellectual defenders of the status quo. Their essentially supportive relationship to the social order is not inconsistent with moderate social criticism and a reform orientation. Indeed, in liberal democracies the existence of what one might describe as contained dissent—that is, a focus on the failures of existing institutions and social arrangements to achieve the values of the dominant culture, and a prescription as to how these values could better be achieved—reinforces both the competitive pluralistic image of society and the other principal values on which the social order and its system of power rest.

Intellectuals who are alienated from the existing order, and who in their work express fundamental criticism of the dominant culture on which that order rests, are, at least potentially, agents of social change. As the term is used here, social change refers to modifications in institutions and social relationships that would have as their consequence the reduction or elimination in the power and privileges of a society's dominant interests and an increase in those of currently subordinate interests. Alienated intellectuals' critique of the dominant culture is linked, at least implicitly, to an alternative social vision. In order for their ideas to become politically relevant, as opposed to remaining a mere underground cultural fringe, they must articulate the grievances and aspirations of social interests that can be mobilized for political action. As Barrington Moore rightly observes, the notion that a vanguard of intellectuals can by the sheer force of their ideas and astute strategy bring about fundamental social change is a fiction, which is due at least partly to the fact that intellectuals write the histories of social developments, and are inclined to project their ego needs onto the canvas of history.[43] Two pre-conditions need to exist for intellectuals to play the role of political vanguard: first, social interests that are either sufficiently numerous (a subordinate class) or else highly cohesive and therefore capable of political mobilization (a subordinate group such as a minority nationality), and that feel excluded from the benefits distributed under the existing social order; and second, an organizational vehicle to mobilize this dissent from the dominant culture. In non-revolutionary societies this usually will be a political party. Adam Przeworski observes that "Political parties–along with unions, churches, factories and schools–forge collective identities, instill commitments, define the interests on behalf of which collective actions become possible, offer choices to individuals, and deny them."[44] It is in this context that intellectuals play an important role in structuring political discourse.

This study focuses on a particular subset of intellectuals, namely, social scientists. More precisely, the following chapters examine the role of social scientists as intellectuals in modern Canadian politics since the time of World War II, including the forms and extent of social scientists' involvement in the political process, their relationship to the state, and the complexities of their class position.

Our choice of the period around World War II as the starting point for this study was dictated by several important factors. One of these was the existence of a number of very good studies on the political involvement of Canadian intellectuals before and during the War. Among the best of these are Doug Owram's *The Government Generation*, J.L. Granatstein's *The Ottawa Men*, and Michiel Horn's *The League for Social Reconstruction*.[45] Owram's masterful study is particularly important, covering the early development of the social sciences in Canada and their contribution to the emergence of the positive state. Two recent works have to some extent bridged the pre-war and post-war periods as their authors attempted the ambitious task of surveying the development of social sciences since Confederation. Marcel Fournier's *L'Entrée dans la modernité: science, culture et société au Québec* examines the development of the social sciences in Quebec through an account of their most famous representatives: Edouard Montpetit, Father Marie-Victorin, Father G.H. Lévesque, Jean-Charles Falardeau, and Paul-Emile Borduas. Douglas V. Verney's *Three*

Civilizations, Two Cultures, One State: Canada's Political Traditions, in contrast to our study, refuses to accept as an organizing principle the notion of Canada's two cultural solitudes. Verney prefers a discussion of the interaction between different political traditions. Our objectives are somewhat less ambitious than those of Fournier and Verney, who both discuss over a century of political traditions and influences.[46]

In the case of Quebec, the emergence of the modern social sciences can be reasonably dated from institutional developments at Laval University and the University of Montreal in 1942–3, foreshadowing the eventual freedom of these disciplines from ecclesiastical influence. The unique institutional development of the social sciences in Quebec and their relationship to Quebec nationalism led us to examine the francophone social science community of this province separately from the predominantly anglophone community in the rest of Canada.

In endeavouring to understand the political significance of social scientists in modern Canada we draw upon a wide range of primary sources and secondary literature. In developing a synthesis of writings and evidence pertaining to this subject, we attempt to provide insights into the more general questions of the role of intellectuals in politics, and the reasons for the differences that have existed between French and English Canada. The study proceeds through three stages:

- An analysis of the role, political discourse and forms of *engagement* of Québécois social scientists, from the institutionalization of the social sciences after World War II to the present.
- An examination of the social sciences in English-speaking Canada, particularly economics and political science, with emphasis on their relationship to the Canadian state and the structure of economic power in Canadian society.
- General conclusions regarding the political role of intellectuals in Canada as a whole and within the province of Quebec.

Our framework of analysis views social science activity in its relationship to larger patterns of social and economic development. In the case of Quebec social scientists, this requires that their relationship to the national question, and to the socio-economic transformations that acquired accelerated force in the 1960s, be the main foci. It is argued that the social sciences in Quebec have passed through three distinct periods of development since World War II. The first, extending until roughly the end of the Duplessis regime in 1959, involved a struggle for the legitimacy of the social sciences within the ideological system of Quebec society, and for the institutionalization of the field. In political terms, these developments paralleled, and were related to, the growing opposition to the so-called "unholy alliance" of the ideologically conservative Union Nationale government, anglophone capital, and the church establishment in Quebec. The advent of the second period coincided with the beginning of the Quiet Revolution and the rapid expansion of the state sector undertaken by the Lesage government. This was a period of growth for the social sciences, during which the secularization of the universities was confirmed and social scientists consolidated their group legitimacy through their contribution to the project of defining the new Quebec and their participation as technocrats within the apparatus of the provincial state. This period of legitimation came to an end at the close of the 1960s, when the declining provincial economy led to strains in the relationship between the state and the predominantly leftist community of social scientists. These strains would be exacerbated in the late 1970s. The increasing gap between the province's revenues and expenditure requirements compelled the Parti Québécois government to take a number of measures which alienated much of the new middle class and the public-sector unions on whose support the PQ depended, and which caused many in the nationalist social science community to reconsider whether the PQ was the appropriate vehicle for the *indépendantiste* project.

In the case of English Canada the relationship of social scientists to politics has been conditioned by a very different set of factors. These include the profound influence of disciplinary developments in the United States on the shape of the social sciences in English-speaking Canada, the dependent structure of the Canadian economy, and the influence of the federal political system which has drawn critical attention to questions of regionalism, constitutionalism, and French-English relations. The colonial origins of the social sciences in Canada, dominated by British or British-trained personnel and by British conceptions of the university and the intellectual enterprise, gave way in the post-war years to American influences; thus, the period from the end of World War II until the early 1960s was characterized by a shift to quantitatively-oriented social sciences. Professional economists enjoyed increasing prominence as the acceptance of Keynesian demand-management expanded the market for their expert skills. By the middle of the 1960s American economic, cultural, and political penetrations of Canadian society had become the foremost issues on the political left, provoking a nationalist response among many political scientists, sociologists and a much smaller number of economists. Even so, social scientists in English Canada were not galvanized by the nationalism issue to the same degree as their colleagues in Quebec; their critical responses took very different, and less effective, forms.

The period from the defeat of the nationalist Waffle movement at the 1971 NDP leadership convention to the present has seen a widening ideological division between segments of the social science community. The nationalist critique of the 1960s contributed to a revival of the political economy tradition in the social sciences, with the important difference that the "new" political economy has been heavily influenced by neo-Marxism, and has been articulated primarily by political scientists and sociologists with very little participation on the part of economists. At the same time, the expert function of the social sciences has continued to gain prominence because of the expansion of analytical capacities within the state (e.g., program evaluation, policy planning, social impact assessment, forecasting), and because rationalism is the language of justification in which most groups feel compelled to express their demands on the state. Analysis and the weight of scientifically-derived evidence have thus become normal elements of political discourse–though their currency should not be confused with influence.

PART ONE

Quebec

The Social Involvement of Intellectuals in Quebec Society: Institutionalization and the Development of a Counter-Ideology, 1943–1960

The following three chapters assume that the ideological role, intellectual discourse, and social involvement of Quebec social scientists, as well as the rise of the social sciences during the 1960s to a position of social prestige and political significance, cannot be fully explained without considering their historical context. Therefore, a brief account of the major events and changes which have occurred in Quebec since World War II, and particularly since 1960, is necessary.

The end of the Second World War is an important point departure in Quebec for a number of reasons. Wartime strengthened Quebec's urban-industrial character, accelerating Quebec's integration into the North American economy and undermining the traditional view of the province as a rural, agrarian, and Church-dominated society. These changes did not have an immediate impact on the political situation. The ideologically conservative Union Nationale Party, under Maurice Duplessis, was in power continuously between 1944 and 1960. During this time the social sciences in Quebec were gaining influence as they made a bid for secular status. Finally, these developments took place in the context of the international reorganization of capitalism and the ascendancy of the American model of social and economic development after World War II.

In 1945 the dominant ideology and political practice in Quebec were still very much at odds with the rest of North America. Urbanization and industrialization were seen as social and national evils, breeding assimilation and the loss of religion; state economic and social intervention were anathema.[1] This ideology postulated a rural, French and Catholic society, resistant to foreign (i.e., Anglo-Protestant) influences. This meant that social services and education in Quebec were left largely in the hands of the church, not the state, as the fundamental social organization. Industrialization, whether in the resource or manufacturing sectors, was left to private initiatives which were either American or English-Canadian. The Quebec ideology maintained that French Canadians' mission in North America was "less to manipulate capital than to manipulate ideas."[2]

It should be recognized that the exclusion of French Canadians from the economic sector had begun immediately after the Conquest, with the replacement of the French *commerçants* by English merchants, and had been reinforced by the defeat of the 1837 rebellion. According to Paul-André Linteau, René Durocher, and Jean-Claude Robert, this domination continued well into the twentieth century: "Quebec society was clearly dominated between 1897 and 1930 by a capitalist class that had substantially increased its power and control over the economy ... It was overwhelmingly English-speaking and concentrated in Montreal."[3]

The question of economic control had not been overlooked by nationalist thinkers, but there were serious obstacles to its solution within the framework of the dominant conservative ideology. This ideology was, structurally speaking, a direct reflection and justification—both legitimization and rationalization—of the socially dominant positions available to French Canadians in Quebec: the clergy, politics, and the liberal professions. It was not disturbed by their relative exclusion from the province's business elite.

The study of Quebec society began to be put on a positivistic basis at Laval and the University of Montreal at a time when the social consequences of urbanization and industrialization had become impossible to ignore. Sociographic and sociological studies brought forth a refutation of the dominant ideology and an indictment of the policies of the Duplessis government. The 1949 Asbestos strike has justly been considered both a "litmus test" of these social changes in Quebec and a catalyst in the emergence of a vast social movement against the old ideology and practice embodied in the Duplessis regime. Social science intellectuals, especially those at Laval University, constituted the ideological vanguard of this social movement. Their development of a counter-ideology was not only a result of greater positive knowledge of society, but also a part of the struggle for the institutionalization of social sciences in Quebec: both a product and an expression of the transformation of Quebec society.

The 1960 election of the Liberal government under Jean Lesage signalled the true beginning of the Quiet Revolution, whose directions had already been debated during Premier Sauvé's "one hundred days." A fundamental shift occurred at the level of the dominant ideology with the acceptance of state economic intervention to both initiate and regulate development; the secularization of social services and education; and the arrival of the social sciences as instruments of social management and modernization.

The historical trend of Quebec nationalism was also reversed. The old emphasis on conserving existing values and institutions against external threats was replaced by criticism of the powers and resources of the Quebec state in the project of *rattrapage* (catching up). The clarion call for a new generation of Québécois became "maîtres chez-nous" as the province was changing socially and politically, and Quebec's economic strategy was embarking on a new course aimed at achieving modernity. The government of Jean Lesage was determined to use the powers of the provincial state to promote rapid economic growth, to facilitate French-Canadian participation in the economy, and to institute policies favourable to the labour movement whose collaboration was essential to the government's objectives of rapid growth. An important series of reforms— the nationalization of the hydroelectric industry, the creation of a ministry of education, the proliferation of state enterprises, and the revamping of labour and social policy—all attested to this ideological and political shift. For social science intellectuals these developments, which expanded the importance of higher education and increased employment opportunities outside of academe, confirmed their social worth. In the provincial public service alone, the number of those with graduate degrees in the social sciences increased from 16 in 1959 to 185 in 1966.[4]

The defeat of the Liberals in 1966 is usually considered the last expression of the Quiet Revolution. Inasmuch as the Union Nationale government under Daniel Johnson tended to consolidate the previous reforms rather than institute new ones,[5] this may be a proper characterization. The Liberals' defeat was a result of the pace of reform, in both directions, in that different segments of the population saw it as moving either too quickly or too slowly. The late 1960s also saw a radicalization of the nationalist movement at the grassroots level, especially on the issue of language; moreover, the economic boom of the 1960s was coming to an end, adding a greater urgency to labour and social issues.[6] On the political fringe this radicalism was expressed in the activities of the Front de libération du Québec (FLQ). Closer to the mainstream, the growing unrest was institutionalized with the founding of the Parti Québécois in 1968.

Since the mid-sixties, Quebec society has been grappling with the consequences and implications of the Quiet Revolution and of entry into the mainstream of North American development. The importance of the national issue, both in the politics of post-Quiet-Revolution Quebec and in the work of Quebec social scientists, largely reflects the dominant ideology's view that the provincial state is the proper forum in which to come to terms with the problems of modernity. During the 1960s and 1970s this Quebec-centred ideology was accompanied by a new emphasis on democratic control of, and participation in, the state. The present

Table 2

Field of Specialization of Graduate Social Scientists Employed by the Quebec
Civil Service, 1955–1966

	Before 1955	1955–9	1960–2	1963–4	1965–6	Total
Economics	1	4	11	27	26	69
Industrial relations	3	1	10	6	20	40
Political Science	1	–	7	9	11	28
Sociology	1	–	3	5	10	19
Social services	1	1	5	7	5	19
No specialty	2	1	2	1	4	10
Total	9	7	38	55	76	185

Sources: Paul Gervais, *Les Diplômés en sciences sociales dans la fonction publique du Québec* (Master's thesis,
Université de Montréal 1970), 66.

demobilization of nationalist forces in Quebec and the dismantlement
of some of the statist legacy of the Quiet Revolution and the state expansion
that took place under the PQ in the 1970s is in part a reflection of a more
general social and political demobilization that has been occurring in
North America and some countries of Western Europe. Of course, what
appears to be a demobilization may well be simply a process of realignment
and reorganization of social forces at the grass-roots level.

It is necessary to uncover the kinds of linkages between the social
developments that Quebec society has undergone and the reflection of
social change in political discourse. This practical application constitutes
the intellectuals' reading of the events described above and also defines
the intellectual and ideological context of subsequent developments. In
general terms, three historic interpretations of Quebec society have been
identified by francophone social scientists, especially by sociologists. The
periodization used by Marcel Fournier and Gilles Houle[7] provides a
useful point of departure. It should be emphasized, however, that their
periodization is based on the *predominance*, not the absolute hegemony,
of a particular characterization of society. The main features outlined
below cannot account for all variations and debates occurring in each
period.

The first period (1943–60) was dominated by the "folk-urban" interpretation, which focused on the problem of tradition versus modernity.
This interpretation, a product of Laval University's Faculty of Social
Sciences (and especially its department of sociology), was based on the
perceived antipathy between the industrialization of Quebec and the
backward-looking institutions and ideology of French Canada, as well

Table 3
Distribution of Graduate Social Scientists in the Quebec Civil Service (Based on University Attended), 1955–1966

	Economics	Industrial Relations	Political Science	Sociology	Social Work	No Declared Speciality	Total	%
Univ. Laval	46	26	19	16	12	5	124	67.0
Univ. Montreal	8	13	2	3	6	–	32	17.3
Univ. Ottawa	4	–	3	–	–	1	8	4.3
Other Canadian universities	2	1	2	–	–	1	6	3.3
American univ.	–	–	1	–	–	1	2	1.1
British univ.	3	–	–	–	–	2	5	2.7
French univ.	4	–	1	–	–	–	5	2.7
Other univ.	2	–	–	–	1	–	3	1.6
Total	69	40	28	19	19	10	185	100.0

Source: Paul Gervais, *Les Diplômés en sciences sociales dans la fonction publique du Québec* (Master's thesis, Université de Montréal 1970), 87.

as on the differences between the ethnic culture and the culture of the English.

Good examples of social analysis during this period are such works as Horace Miner's *Saint-Denis, A French Canadian Parish* (1939); E.C. Hughes's, *French Canada in Transition* (1943); and Jean-Charles Falardeau's *La Rencontre de deux mondes* (1945). This characterization, which was based on studies of specific communities, also achieved expression in the project of *rattrapage*. Ideas of participatory democracy were being proposed in an attempt to bring into this new social project cities and villages, poor and rich, workers and employers. The Bureau d'aménagement de l'Est du Québec, a pilot experience in regional development, provides a good illustration of this effort to include local communities in the general project of *rattrapage*.

The second period (1960–70) was dominated by the idea of Quebec as a dependent nation whose social and economic development had been stunted and distorted by its subordinate relationship to British North America. This interpretation featured (1) the definition of Quebec as a global society (i.e., as an object of analysis in its own right); (2) the continued criticism of the conservative ideology with its unitary view of Quebec; (3) a recasting of the folk-urban continuum in terms of modernization (i.e., in terms of distinctions between pre-industrial, industrial, and post-industrial societies); and (4) a nationalist perspective focused on Quebec instead of "French Canada." Thus, "the object of analysis is no longer 'small communities' but rather Québec as a global society, that is to say a society which has its own economic infrastructure, social structure, state and ideologies, and which, as such, can be the object of specific sociological studies. And this sociological problematic is closely linked to a nationalistic perspective–bringing to light the economic inferiority of francophone Québécois, the political weakness of the Québec state, the process of anglicization ..."[8] In addition to this nationalistic perspective, there existed as an underlying value of the intellectuals' alternative social vision, a belief in democratic socialism based on greater popular participation.

Among the chief contributors to this interpretation were Yves Martin and Fernand Dumont in *L'Analyse des structures régionales* (1963); Gérard Bergeron in *Le Fonctionnement de l'Etat* (1965); Marcel Roux in *La Question du Québec* (1969); Gilles Bourque and Nicole Frenette in "Classes sociales et idéologies nationalistes au Québec 1760-1970" (1970); and Hubert Guindon in "The Social Evolution of Quebec Reconsidered" (1960).

The third period (1970 to present) is dominated by an interpretation based on class analysis. No doubt this is a result of the introduction of Marxist approaches in university teaching and in the intellectual discourse of the social sciences. But it has also followed logically from criticisms of the Dofny-Rioux concept of ethnic class,[9] as well as reaction to the philosophical idealism and impracticality of democratic socialism in the preceding period. In this perspective, Quebec is defined as an incomplete society, inasmuch as its dominant class is not an indigenous one. A more recent formulation of the class analysis interpretation has concentrated on social movements and on autogestion (self-management).

Studies exemplifying the present-day interpretation include Jean-Jacques Simard in *La Longue Marche des technocrates* (1979); Gérard Boismenu, Gilles Bourque, and Daniel Salée, *Espace régional et nation* (1983); Jacques Godbout, *La Participation contre la démocratie* (1983); Gilbert Renaud, *A l'ombre du rationalisme: la société québécoise, de sa dépendance à sa quotidienneté* (1984); and Marc Raboy, *Old Passions, New Visions: Social Movements and Political Activism in Quebec* (1986).

We can conclude with Fournier and Houle that "The construction of these general interpretations [of Quebec society] thus appears as a function of both the social-political conjuncture (and sometimes of particular political events) and of the institutional conditions (and structure of the local intellectual field) in which the sociologists-intellectuals find themselves."[10] These three dominant interpretations, necessarily linked to social developments in the province, provide us with a framework for the analysis of the role, discourse and social involvement of Québécois intellectuals. At the same time, they constitute a set of theoretical categories for the understanding of Quebec society.

Our discussion is divided into two parts. In the first part, we consider the pre-institutional phase of the social sciences and the French-Canadian version of the social doctrine of the Catholic Church, which, as the dominant ideology in Quebec society, determined the theory and practice of these pre-institutions. In the second part, we examine the struggle for institutionalization of the social sciences, independent of church doctrine and control, at Laval University.

Institutionalization is here defined as the process of acquiring the material, the human resources, and the independence necessary for self-regulated intellectual activity. In concrete terms, the indices of this process are the establishment of a departmental structure in the faculties of social sciences, the specialization of the curriculum, and the hiring of a permanent specialized teaching staff. To put this in somewhat different terms, institutionalization involves the formation of a body of permanent specialists whose "training, recruitment, and career are regulated by a specialized organization and who find in the institution the means to establish successfully their claim to a monopoly over the propagation of a legitimate culture."[11]

The Ecole sociale populaire (ESP) of Montreal, founded in 1911; the Semaines sociales du Canada, which began in 1920; the Ecole des sciences sociales, économiques, et politiques of the University of Montreal, founded in 1920; and the Ecole des sciences sociales of Laval University, founded in 1932–all belong to the pre-institutional phase of the social sciences in Quebec. Their basic objectives were to propagate the social doctrine of the church and, in so doing, to combat religious indifference, socialism, communism, and anti-clerical liberalism. Yet, in their different clienteles and in their methods, they were clearly distinct from one another. The Ecole sociale populaire's main target and clientele was the working class. As its first brochure indicated, its purpose was "to work for the people's salvation and the improvement of its lot, by propagating the idea of Catholic association, especially in the professional field. Religious and temporal preoccupations which, oriented especially toward the workers were translated by the concern to organize them."[12]

The ESP, despite its name, was not a school in the proper sense; it was a propaganda office. This was demonstrated by the panoply of its activities: publication of pamphlets and a journal; organization of the Semaines sociales du Canada for conferences and study circles; establishment of a centre for documentation and consultation; and a press service. It constituted a pre-institution, in the sense that it was part of the "pre-sociology"[13] prevalent in Quebec, where the study of social issues was carried on with reference to the social doctrine of the Church– but also in the sense that some of its pamphlets furnished sociographic descriptions of their objects of concern, such as the condition of workers, of the family, etc. The same can also be said of the Semaines sociales; their clientele, however, was broader than that of the ESP, so that the series preferred to address concrete issues and problems within society. As to their method of inquiry and analysis, "to the French Canadian elite of the *Semaines sociales*, sociology was a practical discipline, based on sound philosophy and theology, which studied the doctrine of the social encyclicals and examined data on social problems in the light of the social teachings of the Church."[14] *Rerum Novarum* and *Quadrigesimo Anno* had a profound influence on the teachings of the ESP. Pope Leo XIII's *Rerum Novarum*, issued in 1891, stressed the formation of Catholic labour unions with the goal of eliminating class conflict. It focused on the themes of social justice, charity, and the arbitration of industrial conflict to maintain social harmony. The pursuit of consensus was also central to Pope Pius XI's 1931 encyclical, *Quadrigesimo Anno*. It proposed the creation of *corps intermédiaires*, formal organizations that would group employers and employees under the leadership of the church.

The message of the ESP (after 1949 the Institut social populaire) was articulated around two basic goals for the development of Quebec: Catholic trade unionism to protect the workers from the twin subversions of materialism and religious indifference; and integrative corporatism to achieve the general interests of the nation while preventing social agitation and the subversion of authority. Raymond-G. Laliberté notes that the corporatist theme was dominant and was directly related to the social disorder of the Great Depression.[15] Before we examine the content of these "projets sociaux," it is necessary to examine the basic themes of the church's social doctrine as advocated in Quebec. Pierre Trudeau gives a comprehensive description of these themes: (1) xenophobia towards all that is not Catholic; (2) authoritarianism; and (3) idealism, in that the solutions to the social problems of Quebec are based on abstract reasoning rather than positive knowledge of society.[16] These "solutions," which explicitly or implicitly were part of the church's social doctrine, were agriculturalism, small business, cooperatives, Catholic trade unionism, and corporatism. For Trudeau, the basic fallacy of this doctrine was that the first two themes encouraged the rejection of modernity.

A further indication of the ideological content of this social thought was revealed in the basic elements of the ESP's corporatism. The concept of "corporations" was defined by J.P. Archambault, SJ, a founding member of the ESP, as a "legally constituted body grouping all of the members of the same profession (e.g., laborers, foremen, office workers, managers, owners) under a single authority, having the power to act for the common good and to impose its decisions on all interested parties."[17] In practice, corporatism would include the following features:

1 Unity of doctrine (the Church), of direction (hierarchical organization), and of action (the corporations);
2 Unity of classes as a principle of social harmony;
3 The national arena defined as French Canada in racial (ethnic) terms, and as Quebec in legal-constitutional terms, integrated to the universality of the church;
4 The general interests of the nation defined in terms of the family, the local community, and the corporation under the overarching presence of the church;
5 The corporatist organization of society as either a replacement of the state or as a parallel power, and the concept of the subsidiary role of the state as a non-directive financial supporter of the corporations;
6 Catholic governance: justice (as a source of equity) and Christian charity (as a field of consensus) constitute the ethical grounding of the corporatist organizations;
7 Catholicism as the transcending ideology of corporatism.

The basic themes of the social doctrine, as outlined by Trudeau, are quite evident here. This constituted (with variations of emphasis at different points in time) the dominant ideology and the intellectual environment in inter-war Quebec. It was also the ideological adversary of the movement to institutionalize the social sciences.

The first school of social sciences in Quebec, l'Ecole des sciences sociales, économiques et politiques de Montréal, was founded in 1920 under the direction of Edouard Montpetit.[18] The objective of this school was to further the general work being done by the ESP: to "furnish to the elite and those that social involvement interested, a general culture permitting them to exercise high administrative functions."[19] In fact, however, a program of continuing education was offered (until 1950) only through night courses concentrating on law and political economy. Although the Ecole became a faculty in 1943, it remained a pre-institution until the mid-1950s, when the introduction of day courses leading to a diploma in one of the social sciences and the hiring of a specialized teaching staff were finally achieved. According to Michel Leclerc, the strategy of development during this pre-institutional period was characterized by "a public identification with the dominant ideology of a society whose official agents would never be overtly criticized and an inflexible defense of a mode of social organization more responsive to rules of social equity and political rationality."[20]

The Ecole des sciences sociales at Laval University, founded in 1932, had the same limitations as the Montreal school. Regarding its objectives, Monsignor Roy, then vice-rector of the University, indicated that "Laval University believes that it would be useful to create a center of studies where the principles, the doctrine, the pontifical social directives and experience will jointly enlighten and where those of our fellow-citizens, particularly our young professionals, who can give to the social question a part of their time and of their leisure, will be able to educate and enlighten themselves."[21] As in the case of the Ecole des sciences sociales, économiques et politiques, this goal was pursued through a program of continuing education based on night courses. The reorganization of the Laval school in 1938 under a new director, Father George-Henri Lévesque, OP, was the point of departure for the process of institutionalization.

Though significant, these initiatives did not challenge the prevailing cultural division of labour. Evidence collected by Louis Maheu for the period 1926–35 reveals that the University of Montreal issued 237, 219, and 759 undergraduate degrees in the fields of sciences, engineering, and health, respectively. During the next decade, the numbers were 363, 497, and 1002.[22] In the field of sciences, McGill continued to outdistance both Laval and Montreal during those years. The proportion of diplomas in the sciences granted by Laval and Montreal actually decreased from

29 per cent of all diplomas (55 out of 190) during the period 1926–30 to 16.5 per cent (243 out of 1432) for the period 1946–50.[23]

The representation of French Canadians was concentrated in the liberal professions. For instance, in 1941 francophones comprised 61.5 per cent of surgeons and doctors, 78.7 per cent of lawyers and notaries, and 85.8 per cent of magistrates in Quebec.[24] Table 4 on the federal civil service indicates that French Canadians were almost entirely excluded from scientific positions within the federal state, a fact reflecting the traditional orientation of francophone higher education in Quebec. Selected data for the years 1924 and 1939 demonstrate the extent to which classical college education was skewed in favour of religious studies. Close to 50 per cent of all graduates majored in religion. There is, however, evidence of growing interest in education for a scientific career.[25]

The process of institutionalization which took place between 1938 and 1959 started at Laval with the establishment of regular day courses at the Ecole des sciences sociales leading to a degree in the social, political, and economic sciences. While the teaching was still dominated by Thomist philosophy and the social doctrine of the church, the change was fundamental. As Marcel Fournier remarks, "for the most part without any other university or professional education, these 'new' students, who could well have gone into theology, law or medicine, relied for their future employment prospects, on the value, both intellectual and social, of the diploma they obtained."[26] Thus, apart from religious orthodoxy, a new preoccupation was present in the objectives of the Ecole: that of competence. This was also linked to a shift in the clientele of the Ecole, appealing to those who defined themselves as an elite and who sought positions in the public sector or entry into politics. Among its students, the Ecole attracted some of Quebec's outstanding political leaders, including Arthur Tremblay (member of the Commission of Inquiry on Education), Jean Marchand (a union leader, who held several portfolios under Trudeau's Liberal government), Claude Morin (Quebec Minister of Intergovernmental Affairs, 1976–81), Maurice Lamontagne (economic adviser to the Privy Council, later to become a federal minister), and René Lévesque (Quebec premier, 1976–85). At the same time, the Ecole began a process of social involvement through the founding of the Conseil supérieur de la coopération, the establishment of its journal *Ensemble* in 1938, and the creation of the Centre de culture populaire (dispensing civic and social education) in 1944. One can see in these developments at Laval the two main lines of the strategy of institutional development during this period: first, a gradual and cautious shift toward a positivist social science; and second, the building of a network of alliances with social organizations such as the cooperatives, and later the trade unions, to gain popular support for the school and to establish its social value.

Table 4

Distribution of Scientific Personnel in the Federal Civil Service, by Specialization and Ethnicity, 1930

| | English Canadians | French Canadians | |
Specialization	No.	No.	%
Astronomer	15	0	0
Physicist	26	0	0
Chemist	90	5	5.2
Geologist	43	2	4.5
Zoologist/Entomologist	101	1	0.9
Botanist	69	2	2.8
Naturalist	20	1	4.7
Others	4	0	0
Total	368	11	2.9

Sources: Jacques Rousseau, "Les Sciences pures chez les Canadiens français, *Opinoins* 3, no. 3 (July 1932): 9–10, adapted from Marcel Fournier, *L'Entrée dans la modernité* (Montréal: Editions St. Martin 1986), 94, 111.

In 1943 Laval's Ecole des sciences sociales was transformed into a faculty. The internal reorganization that accompanied this change was fundamental. Its most important aspect was the implementation of a departmental structure (sociology-social ethics, economics, social service, and industrial relations) and of a centre for social research. Concurrent with this structural change and, to a certain extent, necessitated by it, were the specialization of teaching and the hiring of a full-time teaching staff who had been educated in American or Canadian universities. The hiring of a new specialized staff at the Ecole revealed a preference for American-trained professors.

After obtaining a first degree at the Ecole (1938–41), Jean-Charles Falardeau went to the University of Chicago before returning in 1943 as a member of the teaching staff. Following similar careers, Maurice Tremblay and Maurice Lamontagne graduated from Harvard University (in sociology and economics, respectively); Roger Marier received a diploma in social work from Washington University; Albert Faucher, who received a degree in economics from the University of Toronto, joined Fathers George-Henri Lévesque, Gonzalve Poulin and Gilles Lévesque to form the first teaching staff at the Ecole in 1943.[27] Later the faculty experienced further American influence: Guy Rocher obtained his PHD from Harvard in 1958, while Marc-Adélard Tremblay and Gérald Fortin received their doctorates from Cornell University in 1954 and 1956.

Table 5
Classical College Graduates (Quebec)

Career	1924		1939	
	No.	%	No.	%
Religion	201	50.0	308	44.4
Law	51	12.7	41	5.9
Medical profession	90	22.4	119	17.2
Engineering and sciences	25	6.2	103	14.9
Arts and social sciences, Journalism, teaching	8	2.0	24	3.5
Commerce	18	4.5	51	7.4
Others	9	2.2	47	6.7
Total	402	100.0	693	100.0

Source: A. Maheux, "Où vont nos bacheliers?", *L'Action universitaire* no. 5 (January 1940): 19; Claude Galarneau, *Les collèges classiques au Canada français* (Montréal: Fides 1978); Marcel Fournier, *L'Entrée dans la modernité*, 105.

The visit in 1942–3 of Everett C. Hughes, from the University of Chicago–a visit that was linked to the establishment of the Centre of social research–marked the introduction in the curriculum of positivist methods of social inquiry. Falardeau maintains that the change from a normatively oriented social science to a positive applied science was unavoidable, considering that the natural road to Europe was closed due to the war.[28] In any case, these developments were later criticized as contributing to the Americanization of Quebec sociological thought.[29]

The creation of a specialized teaching staff, the introduction of new methods of social inquiry, and the establishment of structures allowing the emergence of a social community within the faculty thus established the preliminary conditions of struggle for legitimacy and autonomy of the fledgling social sciences at Laval. On the Ecole as a social and professional community, Falardeau (who was there at the time) notes: "For the sociologists [sociology rather than the social sciences being his object of analysis], the department in the American style was at the same time a meeting place, a recruitment point, a base of social and political action, and a centre of research concurrently with a professorship."[30] In the face of the dominant conservative ideology in society at large and the religious orthodoxy of the university, these innovations had to be justified. This justification was expressed in Father George-Henri Lévesque's dualist conception of the social sciences. This view had its most forceful expression in his statement to the Canadian Political Science Association in 1947: "As a sociologist, the student is interested only in one thing: to ascertain objectively, dryly, the facts as they are, notwith-standing what philosophy may have taught him to think. After the ac-complishment of his sociological work, it will be time to pass a value judgement on the results of his research, then it will be as a philosopher that he will pronounce himself. *Value judgements can logically come only after judgements of reality.*"[31]

As the 1940s came to an end, the precarious academic status of the social sciences at Laval was guaranteed only by major concessions. The most important of these was the Faculty of Social Science's effective subordination to Thomist philosophy and theology. One proof of the Faculty's orthodoxy, which Father Lévesque did not hesitate to emphasize, was "the still relatively considerable presence of ecclesiastics on the teaching staff."[32] Though their number increased from three to five between 1944 and 1951, their share dropped from one half to one third of the expanded teaching staff.

The 1950s were characterized by an overt struggle between the gov-ernment under Premier Duplessis and the Faculty at Laval, starting with the financial and moral support given by the Faculty to the Asbestos strikers in 1949.[33] Furthermore, the increasing emphasis on research meant that the academic work of social scientists was a direct challenge, not only to the policies of the government, by showing their deficiencies, but also to the premises and solutions advocated under the social doctrine of the church. Lastly, the degree of specialization in the curricula and the hiring of a specialized teaching staff meant the gradual exclusion of those who did not have the required level of specialized knowledge—those who by their education were in the best position to maintain the dominance of Thomist philosophy and the social doctrine of the church. Fournier makes this point when he writes that "the establishment of such a body [of specialists in the social sciences] was not only correlative with the objective dispossession of those who were excluded, i.e., at the end of the 1940s, those who only had a theological, philosophical or juridical education, who found themselves dispossessed of intellectual capital and, in a certain way, disqualifed ... Indeed, the simple fact of constructing Quebec society as an object of research and of introducing in the analysis of any social problem a specialized and, for the most part, esoteric methodology and conceptualization, could only discredit and, by the same token, harm the interests of those who had acquired a monopoly on the power of defining situations: this became a subversive act."[34]

The "subversive" character of the Laval Faculty also found expression in the social involvement of its members. It is known that in the late thirties and in the forties, the Faculty, and especially Father Lévesque, had already been involved in the cooperative movement (the famous issue of confessionality) and in popular education.[35] During the 1950s, the involvement of graduates and of members of the Faculty in the trade union movement, especially the Confédération des travailleurs catholiques du Canada (CTCC) and, of course, in the Asbestos strike, put them clearly in the anti-Duplessis camp. Their participation in the yearly sessions of the Institut Canadien des affaires publiques (ICAP) established in 1954, not only pitted them once more against the government, but also in direct opposition to the Ecole sociale populaire. Jean Marchand, Jean-Charles Falardeau, Léon Dion, Maurice Lamontagne, and Léon Lortie were among those closely associated with ICAP and with the intellectuals' periodical *Cité libre*. Participation in the media, especially through Radio-Canada, also permitted them to carry their message to the population at large. The first major conflict at Radio-Canada (December 1958–March 1959) gave René Lévesque an opportunity for political involvement as he fought for recognition of the union of program producers–which was won.[36] But from the standpoint of intellectuals, their participation in *Cité libre* was probably the most important form of social involvement during the 1950s, due both to the vanguard role played by this journal in the social movement against the Duplessis regime and the dominant ideology, and to the absence at the time of French Canadian academic publications in the social sciences. Thus, for these intellectuals, including Pierre Elliott Trudeau and Gérard Pelletier (as co-editors), along with Jacques Hébert, Marcel Rioux, Pierre Vadeboncoeur, Fernand Dumont, Pierre Juneau, and Jean Lemoyne, *Cité libre* was a forum for both polemical criticism and scientific publications which were in themselves an act of criticism.

The basic philosophical perspective of *Cité libre* was the personalism of two French social Catholics: Jacques Maritain and Emmanuel Mounier, in whose thought the individual is conceived of as the center of spiritual possibilities. From this basic value, democracy and social justice follow as the most appropriate forms of social organization permitting the full realization of the person and his or her spiritual values. Such a view involves the rejection of collective representation (such as nationalism) both as a denial of the individual through the imposition of orthodoxy, and as a denial of the real problems of society, of which the most important is social inequality. These values of democracy and social justice require the participation of citizens in social organizations: political parties, the media, and trade unions. But democratic reform must also, even especially, focus on the state, inasmuch as the state is the main agent for the alleviation of social inequality. The activity of the state envisioned in *Cité libre* was that of social-democratic planning. Nationalism was rejected as reactionary, in view of historical developments toward the greater interdependence of states and societies, federalism was supported as the wave of the future and as a pluralistic and decentralized form of political organization better able to achieve and guarantee personal freedom and the reduction of social inequalities. It was on the basis of this vision of the state and society that Albert Breton, Raymond Breton, Marc Lalonde, Maurice Pinard, Pierre Elliott Trudeau, and others proposed a federalist-individualist option for Canada. In 1964 they published a manifesto entitled "An Appeal for Realism," in which internationalism and individualism were offered as an alternative to nationalism.[37] In the context of Quebec society in the 1950s, such an ideology meant the total rejection of the dominant role of the church in social organizations and of their confessionality; of the social doctrine of the Church as reactionary and authoritarian; of the political mores of the Duplessis regime as a perversion of political freedom; and of Duplessis's provincialist policies as anachronistic.

Another aspect of the struggle between the Laval faculty and the Quebec government concerned funding. From 1943 to 1951, grants from the province represented over 46 per cent of the faculty's budget.[38] These were reduced in 1949, and cut off in the next two years. However, these actions did not bring about either the firing of Father Lévesque as the dean of the faculty or its dismantling. The university was aware of the loss of revenues; but grants from the federal government helped to compensate for this loss.[39] In fact, the faculty association made representations both before the federal Royal Commission on National Development in the Arts, Letters, and Sciences (Massey Commission) and the Quebec Royal Commission of Inquiry on Constitutional Problems (Tremblay Commission), and gave its support for federal grants to post-secondary education in the provinces.[40] We see here another aspect of the strategy of institutional development: the diversification of funding sources.

In 1958 Professor Léon Dion of the Faculty of Social Sciences at Laval University argued in *Cité Libre* that the question of funding is "necessary justice before and above constitutional policy," and indicated the importance for the university not to be "under quasi-exclusive dependence on the federal government as the single external source of funds and discretionary revenue."[41]

It is not irrelevant that Laval's Father Lévesque was a member of the Massey Commission during the years 1949–51. It is also important to remember the complete opposition of the Duplessis government to any federal intervention in what it considered an area of exclusive provincial jurisdiction. Ironically, Trudeau, a leader of *Cité libre*, supported Duplessis on the funding issues.[42] The conflict with the Duplessis government was the high point in the struggle for institutionalization in that it demonstrated the strength of the Faculty in society through the success of its strategy of outside alliances. It also posed the issue of academic freedom in terms of the autonomy of the church from the state.

Institutionalization of the social sciences at the University of Montreal was comparatively effortless, as a result of the earlier Laval experience. Developments in the social sciences at the University of Montreal followed a rather different course, however, in that the strategy of institutional development favoured a perspective of French-Canadian nationalism (albeit modernized) in contradiction to the social preoccupations and the pan-Canadian perspective at Laval.[43] The Equipe de recherches sociales at the University of Montreal, led by Jean-Marc Léger, d'Iberville Fortier, and Camille Laurin, criticized the traditional nationalist elite for not understanding the new, predominantly urban, and industrialized Quebec. Abbé Gérard Dion, a Laval University professor in the Department of Industrial Relations, shared these views. This group had much in common with the *Cité-libristes* in that they wanted Quebec to modernize. Despite a common opposition to the *vieux régime* and its conservative ideology, and a commitment to the modernization of Quebec society, the different paths followed by the social sciences at Laval and the University of Montreal presaged divisions that would become politically significant during the Quiet Revolution and afterwards.

The status of Quebec social scientists was furthered by the establishment of the Massey Commission in 1949; but it was probably the appointment of the Tremblay Commission in 1953 which contributed most to their growing influence. Esdras Minville, director of the Ecole des Hautes Etudes Commerciales (HEC) and dean of the Faculty of Social, Economic, and Political Sciences at the University of Montreal, and Father Richard Arès, S.J., assistant director of the Institut social populaire, were important influences on the Commission's report. In fact, representation on royal commissions would from then on constitute a major channel for the participation of Quebec social scientists in the policy process. This was demonstrated during the 1960s with the appointment of the Laurendeau-Dunton Commission federally, and the Parent, Dumont, and Gendron commissions in Quebec.

During this first period, Quebec social scientists generally occupied a vanguard role by stressing the importance of social change. Liberal-minded intellectuals centered around *Cité Libre*—though not exclusively, as the involvement of André Laurendeau and Jean-Marc Léger with *Le Devoir* so aptly reminds us. They were searching for ways of improving and of making more relevant the message of traditional nationalism for French Canadians. Laurendeau's commitment was particularly note-worthy. His decision in 1942 to join the Ligue pour la défense du Canada, which was created in protest to Mackenzie King's decision to hold a plebiscite on conscription, and his activity as secretary-general for the

Bloc populaire canadien which replaced the Ligue in September 1942, are examples of his political involvement. Traditional nationalists were still very influential at the time, as the publication of the *Tremblay Report* in 1956 indicated. But the challenges coming from the neo-nationalists were increasingly felt within Quebec intellectual circles.

The subsequent period (1960–70) would be one of maturation in Quebec's social sciences, involving increasing specialization of social scientists as teachers, researchers, and experts, and of nationalization of the scientific field as the Quebec-oriented framework that characterized the University of Montreal came to dominate other sociological interpretations.

CHAPTER TWO

Maturation of the Social Sciences and Engagement, 1960-1970

In this chapter and the next we examine concrete manifestations of political intervention by social scientists in Quebec society and situate the evolution of their political discourse in the context of developments from 1960 to 1970. The maturation of the social sciences in Quebec cannot be understood apart from the coming-of-age of society during this period; and the *engagement* of social scientists was an important factor in the rise of social movements, as well as in the structures and ideological positions that they assumed. As our focus is on concrete manifestations of social involvement, the main areas considered in this part of our study relate to technocratic planning, the trade union movement, citizens' groups, political parties, extra-academic intellectual networks (such as *Parti pris*), and government commissions of inquiry.

The process of maturation that continues to this day can be studied under four themes; these reflect a dual process of nationalization of the social sciences and of increasing specialization between, and within, social science disciplines.[1] These processes have unfolded within the context of a double intellectual dependence. First, the Québécois scientific field is dependent: internally, relative to the Canadian scientific field; and externally, due to the international dependence of the Canadian and Québécois fields, especially in relation to American social science.[2] This dependence of the scientific field is, moreover, a reflection of the situation of Quebec society. Thus, Michel Leclerc notes about political science (but this remark can be extended to the social sciences more generally): "Québécois political science attempts to establish its autonomy and cultural legitimacy relative to the *integrative* forces of a monopolist central state, of which it is politically independent (the United States), and the *assimilative* forces of a peripheric state to which it is politically associated."[3] Second, the international dependence already noted is the case for Québécois social science relative not only to the United States but also to

Table 6
Place of Study of Québec Francophone Political Scientists, 1969–1979 (based on most recent degree)

| | Laval | | | | U. of Montreal | | | | U. of Quebec at Montreal | | | | Total | | | |
| | 1969 | | 1979 | | 1969 | | 1979 | | 1969 | | 1979 | | 1969 | | 1979 | |
	No.	%	No.	%	No.	%	No.	%	No.	%	No.	%	No.	%	No.	%
United States	2	30.7	4	18.2	–	–	1	5.3	1	14.3	3	14.3	5	16.2	8	13.0
France	3	23.1	8	36.4	8	72.7	9	47.4	2	28.6	9	42.8	13	42.0	26	42.0
Belgium	–	–	2	10.6	1	9.1	2	10.6	–	–	1	4.8	1	3.2	5	8.1
Switzerland	2	15.4	2	10.6	1	9.1	2	10.6	1	14.3	2	9.5	4	12.8	6	9.6
United Kingdom	1	7.7	1	4.5	1	9.1	1	5.3	–	–	2	9.5	2	6.4	4	6.4
Quebec	3	23.1	1	4.5	–	–	3	15.5	3	42.8	2	9.5	6	19.4	6	9.6
Canada	–	–	3	13.7	–	–	1	5.3	–	–	1	4.8	–	–	5	8.1
Other	–	–	1	4.5	–	–	–	–	–	–	1	4.8	–	–	2	3.2
Total	13	(100)	22	(100)	11	(100)	19	(100)	7	(100)	21	(100)	31	(100)	62	(100)

Source: Michel Leclerc, *La Science politique au Québec* (Montréal: L'Hexagone, 1982), 207.

the French social sciences. This double dependence is expressed in two ways: structurally, in the need to acquire the necessary professional qualifications outside of Quebec; and intellectually, in the adoption and adaptation of theoretical frameworks and methodological tools developed elsewhere.[4] The preceding table pertaining to the academic training of Quebec political scientists clearly demonstrates, for the period 1969–79, the structural dimension of this dependence. Nearly 80 per cent received their last university degree outside of Canada. Moreover, there is a clear bias in favour of specialists who received their training from France, as they consistently outnumber those trained in English Canada and the United States.

In order to counter this dependence on external sources of training and ideas, intellectuals working in the dependent country often have been supportive of nationalistic measures. By defining the standards of intellectual work and creating their own instruments, including professional organizations and journals, for the diffusion and exchange of this work, Quebec's intellectuals have been able to avoid direct competition with their better-staffed and better-equipped Canadian and American counterparts. Thus, the nationalization of their intellectual community has been in part a self-interested strategy for expanding the opportunities for intellectual recognition and career advancement. To a certain extent, "the condition of the nationalization of a scientific field is its 'étatisation' or at least the more frequent and regular intervention of the state in the sectors of education and scientific research."[5]

Before examining the concrete manifestations of this strategy of nationalization, the changing social context within which it was pursued needs to be emphasized. With the end of the Duplessis regime the forces of modernization were given their opportunity. The result was an expansion of the provincial state as it assumed functions previously performed in the private sector, generally under the aegis of the Church.[6] Academics and social scientists generally were no longer on the outside, ranged against a government that was the embodiment of a social order in which their status was low. With the transition from the conservatism of the Duplessis period to the modernizing rhetoric and actions of the Quiet Revolution, the ideological function passed from the ecclessiastics to the secular intellectuals. Intellectuals were no longer to be found on the barricades, as in opposition to the Duplessis regime during the 1950s, but in commissions of inquiry, planning boards, and halls of government.

The contributions of Quebec social scientists to commissions of inquiry are particularly noteworthy. Surely of foremost importance was their participation in the Quebec Royal Commission of Inquiry on Education (Parent Commission) in 1961 and, at the federal level, the Royal Commission on Bilingualism and Biculturalism (Laurendeau-Dunton Commission) in 1963. The Parent Commission, presided over by Mgr Alphonse-Marie Parent (Vice-Rector of Laval University), gave a solid push to the process of maturation of the social sciences in Quebec by recommending the creation of a Ministry of Education. Quebec's Ministry of Education was established, with Paul Gérin-Lajoie as its first minister, in the following year. This led the way to the passage in March 1966 of an Order in Council for the implementation of pre-university and advanced technical instruction in the Collèges d'enseignement général et professionnel (CEGEPs). A main pillar of the Church's social authority was eroded with the secularization of Quebec's school system.[7] Members of the Parent Commission (1961–6) included Gérard Filion of Le Devoir and later head of the Société générale de financement; Guy Rocher, a prominent sociologist, first at Laval (1952–60) and then at the University of Montreal; and Arthur Tremblay, who (with his Master's degree in education from Harvard), after being appointed associate director of Laval's Ecole de pédagogie served on the Tremblay Commission, and in 1964 became Quebec's first Deputy Minister of Education.

The Laurendeau-Dunton commission was established in July 1963, to make recommendations on English-French relations in Canada. The representation of social scientists, including a number from Quebec, on the commission was considerable, to say nothing of their extensive participation in the research carried out for the commission. Its co-presidents were themselves social scientists: André Laurendeau (first secretary-general for the Bloc Populaire and editor of Le Devoir) and Davidson Dunton (former president of CBC and president of Carleton University between 1958–72), Gilles Lalande (Montreal), Blair Neatby (Carleton), Kenneth McRae (Carleton), John Meisel (Queen's), André Raynauld (Montreal), and Donald Smiley (Toronto). Other social scientists included political scientists Michael Oliver of McGill and Léon Dion of Laval, who were appointed, respectively, director and associate director of the research division. The involvement of Quebec social scientists in the Bilingualism and Biculturalism Commission contrasted sharply with their remote interest in earlier federal commissions: a case in point was the Rowell-Sirois Commission (1939), in which only two French Canadians, Esdras Minville, a political economist (later director of the HEC), and Léon Mercier Gouin, a lawyer, prepared studies under its auspices.

The involvement of social scientists in the experience of regional development, as in the case of the Bureau d'aménagement de l'Est du Québec (BAEQ) was also indicative of their increasing important role as "definers" of society. Political scientists Guy Bourassa, Vincent Lemieux, and Léon Dion, sociologists Guy Coulombe and Gérald Fortin, geographers Guy Lemieux and Lucie Parent, and economist Jean-Claude Lebel were, in various capacities, influential.

Two of these, Guy Coulombe, a former president of the SGF, Quebec Secretary to the Cabinet, and former president and chief executive officer of Hydro-Québec (resigned in December 1987), and Jean-Claude Lebel, also a former president of the SGF and a former secretary of the Treasury Board, occupied important positions of influence in the higher echelons of the Quebec state. At another level, the Quebec Planning and Development Council (COEQ) was also counting on social scientists for their expertise. The influences of economist Roland Parenteau (COEQ director) and of the Deputy Minister of Education, Arthur Tremblay, and the Deputy Minister of Industry and Commerce Michel Bélanger, were particularly felt. These forms of *engagement*, all of which were focused on the state, reinforced the nationalist direction of the social sciences in Quebec, as illustrated in their intellectual discourse and professional structures.

The direct involvement of social scientists as politicians was particularly evident during this phase of maturation and continued engagement (1960–70). At the provincial level, there has been a tendency among intellectuals to join left-leaning independentist parties. The case of Jacques-Yvan Morin, a professor of international law who later went on to occupy the positions of Minister of Education, Minister of State for Cultural and Scientific Development, and Minister of Intergovernmental Affairs during the 1976–85 PQ administrations, illustrates this point. Other cases include André d'Allemagne, a teacher and translator, and Marcel Chaput, a chemist, who led the Rassemblement pour l'indépendance nationale (RIN), which they co-founded in September 1960 with a view to building a secularized, independent Quebec with a social democratic orientation. It is worth noting here that the members of the RIN and *Parti Pris* pursued the same objectives: independence, secularization, and socialism. Pierre Bourgault, a journalist and political analyst, provided a rejuvenated leadership to the RIN as he went on to defend Quebec's right to self-determination, while pushing to the limits the goals of socialism, independence, and secularization.

It was as a journalist and political analyst that René Lévesque first became known and respected in Quebec. In his quest for social change, Lévesque joined the Liberals of Jean Lesage and rapidly became a strong proponent for state interventionism. Finding himself on the left of the party on most issues, and committed to achieving independent status for Quebec, Lévesque eventually decided to quit the Quebec Liberal party, becoming the first leader of the Parti Québécois in 1968. Meanwhile, a social scientist destined for prominence in provincial politics, Robert Bourassa, gained a certain reputation within the ranks of the Quebec Liberal Party as a professor of taxation and finance. In 1963 Bourassa was appointed research director of the Bélanger Commission on provincial finances. According to Don and Vera Murray, Bourassa participated in the preparation of the 1967 Option-Québec document, which brought about a major confrontation during the Liberal party congress of that year and led to the departure from the party of René Lévesque. By the Murrays' account, Bourassa left the pro-Lévesque group at the latest possible moment.[8]

The case of Maurice Lamontagne provides another clear example of a social scientist's effort to influence the course of contemporary politics. After publishing a seminal study, *Le fédéralisme canadien*, in 1954 Lamontagne left his position as professor of economics at Laval University to become a senior bureaucrat with the federal government. The same year he was appointed Assistant Deputy Minister of Northern Affairs and Natural Resources. In 1955 he was named economic advisor to the Privy Council. In 1957 he returned to academe as professor of economics at the University of Ottawa, before being appointed economic advisor to Lester B. Pearson in 1958. He returned to the University of Ottawa in 1961 in the capacity of Assistant Dean of the Faculty of Social Sciences. In 1963, he was elected to the House of Commons, and appointed Secretary of State and Registrar General of Canada in February 1964.

It is noteworthy, however, that few Quebec social scientists followed Lamontagne's career pattern–travelling through the ranks of Ottawa's well-entrenched anglophone bureaucracy. The cases of Pierre Elliott Trudeau, Gérard Pelletier, Jean Marchand, Marc Lalonde, and several others, suggest that the electoral-political road was a more successful path to participation in federal policy making. In fact, the joint decision of Trudeau, Pelletier, and Marchand to enter federal politics was associated with a desire to transform the federal state from an anglophone institution into one providing real opportunities for participation and identity for French Canadians. The trio quickly became known as the Three Wise Men (*Les Trois Colombes*). Trudeau's influence certainly has been greatest. In 1969 his first government introduced the Official Languages Act, in an attempt to silence Quebec nationalists. The latter saw this initiative as merely a way to ensure the further assimilation of the francophone population in Canada. Far from being placated, Quebec nationalists continued mobilizing, this time around the *indépendantiste* Parti Québécois. From its inception the PQ was a party of intellectuals,[9] and would eventually represent Quebec's own version of the French Third Republic's "République de professeurs."

One sign of maturation and nationalization in the social sciences was the creation of a locally controlled system of intellectual production and diffusion through university curricula, publications, journals, colloquia, and learned associations. Illustrative of this increasingly dense network of Quebec-centred intellectual activity was the founding of *Recherches sociographiques* in 1960 at Laval University and of *Sociologie et sociétés* in 1969 at the University of Montreal (and later of *Les Cahiers du socialisme* in 1978 at the University of Quebec, and of *Politique* by the Société Québécoise de science politique in 1982). In their introductory editorial, Fernand Dumont and Jean-Charles Falardeau of *Recherches sociographiques* state as their main objectives the study of Quebec society, as well as the study of other societies in order to provide comparative insights into the Quebec case. This, they indicate, is to be done from a positivist-monographical perspective and in a multidisciplinary context.[10] Dumont's commitment to research was furthered with the establishment in 1966 of Laval's Institut supérieur des sciences humaines which had an interdisciplinary orientation under his direction and produced several important studies on the development of ideologies, social classes, and the processes of social transformation in Quebec. In *Sociologie et sociétés*, Jacques Dofny identifies the main concerns of the journal as: (1) theoretical sociology, defined as the expression of the science attained in dominant countries, to be enriched by its critical use in the study of other societies; (2) the study of Quebec as a special object of analysis based on the questions of nationalism, modernization, and the meeting of different cultures; (3) a stricter emphasis on sociological, rather than multidisciplinary, works; and (4) an emphasis on thematic research, thus encouraging both comparative works and external contributions.[11]

Related to the distribution of these instruments for intellectual communication was the nationalization of learned associations. An exception that predated this period was the Association canadienne française pour l'avancement des sciences (ACFAS), established in 1923 and structured around the promotion of the French language. The organization of scholarship on a nationalist basis became common in the 1960s. Thus, in 1961, the Association canadienne des sociologues et anthropologues de langue française was established as independent of the Canadian Association of Sociologists and Anthropologists. While this was indeed an act of nationalization, it did not sever the links to the Canadian sociological profession, as indicated by the refusal in 1973 to change the adjective "canadienne" to "québécoise." Similarly, in 1964, the Société canadienne de science politique was established as an entity separate from the Canadian Political Science Association. Later, in May 1979, its members voted to change its name to the Société québécoise de science politique. We thus find in the scientific field a replication of the political debate of the 1960s, between independence and the less extreme position of a *statut particulier* for Quebec. This parallel was not coincidental, but was in fact related to developments in Quebec society and the provincial state.

The explosive growth of the Quebec state during the 1960s has been described too often to require recounting here.[12] There is general agreement

Figure 1

Laval University Envolment at the Faculty of Social Sciences, 1938–1984

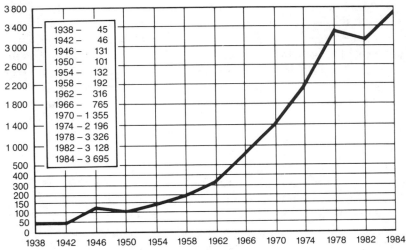

1938 –	45
1942 –	46
1946 –	131
1950 –	101
1954 –	132
1958 –	192
1962 –	316
1966 –	765
1970 –	1 355
1974 –	2 196
1978 –	3 326
1982 –	3 128
1984 –	3 695

Source: Université Laval, Faculté des sciences sociales, *Annuaire 1984–85: Études de premier cycle.*

be one of the only sources of job openings for the growing proportion of that social scientists were instrumental to, and beneficiaries of, the growth of the provincial state.[13] Graduates from social science faculties easily found work in the burgeoning state apparatus. As specialists in economics, political science, industrial relations, sociology, and social psychology (to name but a few disciplines), these new graduates formed the modernist cadres needed to staff the structures of a state that was busily catching up with the North American mainstream.[14] The effects on the faculties of social sciences at Laval and Montreal were considerable. As the social utility of such fields of study increased, they attracted an ever-increasing number of students. Absolute enrolment in these faculties grew rapidly from the early 1960s to the late 1970s.

As the Quiet Revolution progressed, social science professors and specialists rose in status and popular esteem. Their ideological function was to legitimate the policies of the provincial state with either neo-liberal (welfare statism) or social-democratic (planning-interventionist) rhetoric.[15] Jean-Jacques Simard has gone so far as to call this new generation of social scientists Quebec's own version of the Comtean Priests of Humanity.[16] This analogy is not too far-fetched, given that the modernizing nationalism of these members of the university-educated middle classes, who often ascended to high administrative positions in the Quebec public and para-public sectors, had created the new dominant ideology. As Marc Renaud observes: "Given that the [Quebec] state turned out to

Figure 2

Laval University Master's and Doctoral Enrolment at the Faculty of Social Sciences, 1938–1984

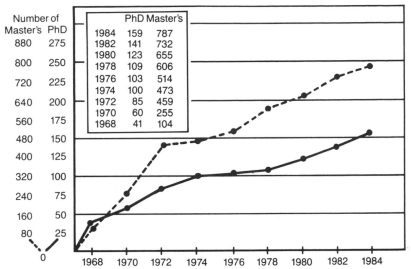

	PhD	Master's
1984	159	787
1982	141	732
1980	123	655
1978	109	606
1976	103	514
1974	100	473
1972	85	459
1970	60	255
1968	41	104

Source: Université Laval, Faculté des sciences sociales, *Annuaire 1984–85*: Études des deuxième et troisième cycles.

university graduates among the French-speaking population, had the civil service and the public sector not expanded, the gap between English- and French-speaking Quebecers would have continued to widen, since the already scarce upper- and middle-echelon jobs of the private economy were closed to the francophones ... University- or technically-trained francophones can in fact be said to constitute a class in the sense that their academic capital provides them with commonly shared levels of market capacity and with a set of objective common interests in seeing the state evolve, by various means, interesting (i.e., prestigious, powerful, and well paid) jobs for them."[17]

Several of the people trained during the pilot experience of development in the Eastern Quebec area, the 1963–6 BAEQ experiment, are now to be found in the upper echelons of the Quebec state. Guy Coulombe and Jean-Claude Lebel were mentioned earlier; other prominent examples of the university-educated middle class which moved into the expanding provincial state include Pierre Martin, who became president of the new provincially-owned energy company. Société québécoise d'initiatives pétrolières (SOQUIP), and Louis Bernard, who until December 1985 was both Secretary-General of Quebec and Clerk of the Executive Council.

So important were these new social scientists in the restructuring of Quebec society that as early as 1964 Philippe Garigue, then Dean of the

Faculty of Social Sciences at Montreal, saw the social sciences, and sociology in particular, as instruments for national development.[18] He wrote: "The very rapid development of sociology at present, as an academic discipline in French Canada, can be explained by the manner in which this discipline became an instrument of national development. The same can be said of all the other social sciences which became more important sources of ideological reflection on the subject of French Canada and whose specialists are among the most active members of the new French-Canadian elite."[19] The growing social and political importance given to the human or social sciences had profound effects on the internal structure and development of these disciplines. These developments related to both the institutional structure of Quebec social sciences and their ideological content.

In Quebec during the 1960s, the social sciences in general went through a period of nationalization.[20] On the one hand, the social sciences faculties at Montreal and Laval received greater funds from the provincial government for all fields of research; on the other hand, these disciplines became increasingly focused on Quebec society as a unique and specific object of analysis. Regarding the funding issue, Marcel Fournier and Louis Maheu point out that research support for the social sciences is affected by Canadian federalism. Over time, provincial financial support for scientific research has been oriented increasingly toward the planning and management of human resources. It is thus not surprising to find that the Quebec government in 1972–3 and 1973–4 was the major funding agent for the social sciences in that province, though the federal government was the principal funding source for research and development in the natural sciences.[21]

Fournier and Maheu argue that this difference in financing emphasis, and the provincial state's more active role in funding social science research, were crucial factors in the nationalization of these disciplines. Table 7 reveals a significant imbalance between the number of professionals in the employ of the Quebec versus the federal government, engaged in research and development and specializing in either social or natural sciences. This imbalance parallels the different emphasis of the federal and Quebec governments regarding funding for these two types of scientific research.

Furthermore, the nationalist rhetoric that one finds in much Quebec social science during this period may plausibly be understood as, in part, a self-interested strategy. In order to consolidate the gains in professional and social status they had made, and to support their claims on public resources, Quebec social scientists had to establish alliances with other social groups which sought an increase in statist activities within Quebec society.

Table 7

Scientists Engaged in Research and Development in the Natural and Social Sciences, Quebec and Federal Governments, 1972–1973

| | Quebec | | Canada | |
	No.	%	No.	%
Natural sciences	432	56.18	5,475	84.91
Social sciences	337	43.82	973	15.09
Total	769	100	6,448	100

Source: Conseil de la politique scientifique du Québec (AREQ 1974), 86.

The creation of funding agencies and several research centres by the Quebec government in the late 1960s, following the recommendations of the COEQ, was welcomed by the province's social scientists. The establishment of a program for research training (Formation de chercheurs et action concertée, or FCAC) in 1969, the creation of the Centre de recherche industrielle du Québec (CRIQ), the Institut de recherche en électricité du Québec (IREQ), and the Institut national de recherche scientifique (INRS), together indicated a firm intention by the provincial government to provide greater support for both the social and natural sciences.[22] As long as the provincial government remained the main supplier of research money, so that expansion in professional and research opportunities was partly dependent on the growth of the state, there existed an objective alliance of interests between social scientists and other groups within the new state-oriented middle class. In fact, the prevalent rhetoric of national liberation espoused by social scientists during the 1960s performed an essential ideological function for the new middle class as a whole–namely, to help it legitimate its claim to speak for and represent the new Quebec.

Changes in the perspectives of social scientists due to the nationalist movement began to be felt when a reinterpretation of the causes of Quebec's stunted development, put forth by Michel Brunet, Guy Frégault, and Maurice Séguin, became widely accepted . These historians contended that the root cause of Quebec's economically backward status was the Conquest of 1760, and the ability of Quebec's anglophone elites to dominate the commerce of Lower Canada and thereby impede the development of an indigenous and secular francophone bourgeoisie. Brunet, Frégault, and Séguin believed that a political solution, in the form of an interventionist Quebec state, could rectify two centuries of economic inequality.[23]

This new historical interpretation did not go unnoticed in sociology. Beginning with Philippe Garigue at McGill, Quebec's sociologists and anthropologists criticized the previously dominant view that Quebec's backward status in North America was the product of its "folk" mentality.[24] In opposition to this cultural analysis, which had been derived from the anthropological theories of Everett C. Hughes and the "Chicago School," the new generation of researchers began searching for social and economic reasons for Quebec's backward economic status. This shift in perspective was all the more important because it joined the national question to the social class question. As Marcel Fournier and Gilles Houle argue, this unification of nationalism and class analysis was the basis for members of Quebec's intelligentsia becoming militants for separatism or socialism, or both.[25]

Quebec's sociologists no longer studied French Canada. Rather, their focus and interests were guided by a will to understand *Le Québec*. Their nationalism was not *just* a political ideology, to be incorporated into party platforms. This ideology, which became the socially dominant interpretation of Quebec society and its relationship to Canada, operated so as to structure the intellectual orientation, methods, and course of social scientific practice itself.

Quebec sociology developed along different lines from Anglo-Canadian and American work of the same period, especially in its use of macro-sociological analyses.[26] This distinctive orientation started from the premise of Quebec's dependent status in North America, and emerged out of social scientists' self-definition as agents for social change and collective liberation. By carving out for themselves a particular and exclusive object-domain to study, Quebec's social scientists were able to achieve a degree of professional and intellectual independence from both the international and Canadian scientific communities. Several prominent francophone academics seem to have been uncomfortable with this situation. Both Philippe Garigue and Fernand Ouellet eventually left for York University, Maurice Pinard went to McGill; and Marcel Trudel went to the University of Ottawa. But the increasingly distinct character of Quebec social science cannot be analyzed solely at the level of internal (i.e., theoretical) developments. To emphasize the point, the Quebec acquisition of a distinctive orientation was helped by the growth of the Quebec state as a funding agent[27] and by the participation of social scientists in the fields of planning, party politics, and extra-parliamentary social movements, all of which lent an *engagé* flavour to their intellectual discourse. Therefore, this process was linked to, and dependent on, the rise of Quebec's new middle class as a dominant force in cultural and political affairs.

Evidence of the self-importance and sense of a nationalist mission among the ideological spokespersons of the new middle class can be found in the analyses made by sociologists on power, elites, social change, and ideologies in modern Quebec.[28] At the level of ideology, the treatment of these subjects by Quebec's sociologists testifies to the privileged position they sought for themselves as social agents of change. For example, at a joint Laval-Montreal symposium on power, organized by *Recherches Sociographiques* in 1966, Fernand Dumont defined power in modern societies as based functionally upon the monopoly control over the production of knowledge.[29] Such an idealized notion of social power might be of questionable validity; certainly it was self-serving in so far as it claimed for the intellectual fraction of Quebec's new middle class the key role in the Quiet Revolution.[30] Also prevalent at this time was the view, expounded by Fernand Dumont, Guy Rocher, and Marcel Rioux, that ethnic elites occupied a strategic position as definers of dominant ideologies. If social power was based on knowledge, and the intellectuals within an ethnic community were understood to be strategically important as ideologists, then it followed that the battle to modernize Quebec would be won or lost at the level of ideas. For these social scientists a monopoly over knowledge also meant control over values, with a view to changing the prevailing social order. Thus, in a period of transition from the social dominance of the traditional elites to that of the new middle class, some social scientists saw themselves as major players in the general reorganization of Quebec society.[31]

But already during this period, after the deceiving attempt at strategic regional planning initiated by the BAEQ (1963–6),[32] certain sociologists were becoming aware of emerging conflicts, on one hand between technocrats and popular elites and, on the other, between central planners and the inhabitants of various regions. There was a growing fear that the centralizing tendencies of statist planning would undermine the development of democratic forms of participation.[33] But as Jean-Jacques Simard has argued, local resistance did not deter the centralizing aims of the new provincial technocrats. To accommodate and contain local protests, both the Liberal and the Union Nationale governments established local and regional councils for consultation. While the official purpose of these councils was to further popular participation in regional planning, they actually brought about the co-optation of regional elites and the further concentration of decision making in Quebec City. Instead of decentralizing the process, such initiatives increased the presence of bureaucrats at all levels of society, in effect extending technocratic domination.[34] Thus, the initial hopes of the early 1960s to modernize Quebec along democratic lines were dashed by the realities of implementing state-centred solutions. The imperatives of bureaucratic control and self-interest undermined the possibilities for democratic control of the *patrimoine*. In this process of technocratization, the administrative work force within the public and para-public sectors profited disproportionately from the growth of the state apparatus.

The professional maturation of the social sciences required the separation of the academic from his or her social role–except in the capacity of expert, an institutionalized and professionally legitimate form of social involvement. The remainder of this chapter examines extra-academic forms of social involvement: specifically, technocratic planning and *animation sociale*; the role of the intellectuals in the trade union movement; and the intellectual network centred on the journal *Parti pris*.

In the field of state planning the fundamental development, which set the stage for others and established the framework of debate on the consequences of planned development was the creation in 1963 of the Bureau d'aménagement de l'Est du Québec (BAEQ). Its object was to promote the economic and social development of eastern Quebec through a combination of planning and democratic participation. Using *animation sociale* techniques (for example, information and community work, leadership training, organization of sectorial committees to study the economic structures of the Eastern Quebec's area, etc.), the BAEQ's goals involved the modernization of the regional economy traditional sectors (agriculture, fishing, and forestry), the training or retraining of workers affected by government economic restructuring programs, and the expansion of economic activities in urban centers to handle migration from rural areas. This pilot project in regional development was part of the *rattrapage* of the 1960s. Gabriel Gagnon notes the importance of the BAEQ for sociologists and other social scientists: "On the one hand, it constituted in Quebec one of the first forms of applied research on a large scale, involving, in one way or another, a large segment of the Québécois sociologists of that time and, on the other hand, in attempting, through *animation sociale*, to establish links with the population, it was trying in its way to detect potential social movements and to facilitate their emergence."[35] It should be noted, however, that this assessment tends to overemphasize the attention given to the population.

Planning and participation involved the abstract goals, the concrete instruments and, to a large extent, the ideology of the BAEQ and those working for it. The basic themes of the planning dimension were (1) the functional and productive integration of resources, population, and forms of socio-economic organization; (2) the transformation of the local traditional and rural mentalities into urban industrial mentalities through animation sociale; and (3) popular acceptance of the framework of planning through the establishment of administrative and territorial structures. The main themes of participation were (1) popular education through participation, as a necessary condition for the successful functioning of the structures established under the plan; (2) *animation sociale* to promote the emergence of new mentalities and of new local leaders; (3) consultation and exchange of information between state technocrats and the people;

and (4) regionalization, that is, the setting up of an intermediary administrative structure between the central (provincial) and the local levels.[36]

These themes, focusing on the state and popular participation, reflect the close connection between technocratic planning and *animation sociale*, on the one hand, and the general ideology of *rattrapage* on the other. Moreover, together they formed the basis for an ideological and practical struggle between the traditional community elites (local, provincial, and federal politicians, the clergy, small and medium businessmen) and the new technocratic elite.[37] Furthermore, it can be seen that the BAEQ's activity was intended to be essentially of an integrative and directive nature. Thus participation and *animation sociale* became a double-edged sword. Although the objective of bringing the local population into the planning process was effectively dominated by the central bureaucracy, it led to popular pressure for real participation.

While the BAEQ's initiatives were directed towards the less densely populated areas of eastern Quebec, *animation sociale* was also occurring in the cities, where it was oriented toward community development.[38] The objectives of its urban activities included improvement of the physical and social environment, the coordination of resources, and the creation of a new leadership.[39] The main differences between this urban *animation sociale* and that taking place in the rural setting were: (1) the greater emphasis in the cities on social services; (2) a more localized focus of intervention (*quartiers*); and (3) a broader base for social intervention. In the 1970s the social service functions of urban *animation sociale* were taken over by the state, with the creation of centres locaux de services communautaires (CLSCs). The social scientists who served as *animateurs* (social activists) were confronted with the choice of finding new occupations or becoming integrated into the state bureaucracy. (A radicalized faction developed out of the urban *animation sociale*, whose focus was the working class at the factory level; this development is discussed in the next chapter, in examining the Centre de formation populaire.)

The basic problems encountered in the context of urban *animation sociale* were: (1) the issue of resources, which came down to a choice between accepting government funding, with the restrictions this carried, and the risk of not being able to have an impact on the community because of insufficient financial resources; (2) the diversity of popular groups both on a functional and issue basis and in terms of ideology, and the resulting difficulties in establishing common fronts leading to the emergence of a politically influential social movement (the failure of the Front d'action politique [FRAP] and the difficulties of the Montreal Citizens' Movement [MCM] until the election of 1986 are examples of this); and (3) the role of the social activists in the popular groups as agents of integration or of radical change.

The BAEQ and similar attempts to stimulate social change reflected and reinforced the increasing status of the social scientist as an expert whose knowledge and skills had concrete social applications. The social scientist as social activist constituted a challenge to the traditional intellectuals (clergy, local notables, parliamentarians) in the rural setting. But the attempt by this group within the new middle class to impose its planning ideology, and the lack of immediate positive results from *animation sociale*, undermined any possibility which might have existed for an alliance with popular rural groups. These groups were becoming very suspicious of government initiatives in the field of regional development, as there was growing evidence that the rural municipalities were not benefiting from this restructuring: rural migration toward urban centers was being accentuated and rationalization of economic activities tended to favour these same urban centers. Regional opposition to planned development mounted.

In the urban setting, the *quartier* character of the interventions in poor communities produced problems of inefficiency in terms of results and integration. Added to this, the more rapid and intense politicization of the issues involved, reflecting both the greater competition between the intellectuals for the paid positions available and the greater political density of the urban setting (in intellectual, educational, and information networks), contributed to criticism of the role of urban social activists and of their administrative and ideological relationship to the state.

Involvement in the trade union movement had been part of the *engagement* of Laval's social science intellectuals, symbolized in their support of the striking workers at Asbestos in 1949. In 1960 the Confédération des travailleurs Catholiques du Canada (CTCC) abandoned its confessional character and became the Confédération des syndicats nationaux (CSN). The elimination of church influence meant the demise of the role of the traditional intellectuals in the labour movement–though admittedly, their influence had steadily declined during the 1950s. The new organization had the advantage of good relations between the Liberal provincial government and its leaders, expecially during Jean Marchand's tenure as head of the CSN (from March 1961 to June 1965), and CSN membership expanded rapidly with the growth in the public sector. Thus, it can be said that the CSN shared in the general ideology of the Quiet Revolution and profited from it. The Fédération des travailleurs du Québec (FTQ), with its largely international character and a membership less oriented to the provincial state, focused its recruitment efforts on the industrial sector and thus was not as capable as the CSN of benefiting from expansion of the state sector during the early 1960s.

The mid-1960s saw a convergence of the ideological positions of the two unions, and the adoption by each of a more critical stance toward the provincial government. In part, this resulted from their disillusionment with the slowing pace of reform. The CSN laid stress on the concept of the working class, criticizing capitalist society as inherently anarchic and unjust, and advocating what it considered to be a truly democratic social order grounded on participation at all levels. "This participation can be realized through decentralization and the control of decision-making by the members of the union, by union action and its participation in the decision-making at the level of the enterprise, through cooperation and the organization of consumers at the level of the economy, and at the political level."[40]

The CSN's ideology of participatory democracy involved a class dimension, identifying workers as the popular classes and considering employers as class adversaries. This new ideological position of Quebec's largest labour organization, although it expressed Marxist concepts, defined itself as reformist in strategy and as anti-dogmatic in theory under the banner of internal union democracy. As Louis-Marie Tremblay notes, the emphasis on internal democracy freed the CSN from the previous dominance of the new intellectuals—a fact demonstrated by the working-class origin and internal succession of its leaders.[41] Marchand's departure in 1965 to enter federal politics provided the opportunity for a new direction in the CSN's leadership. His successor, Marcel Pépin, took it upon himself to reinvigorate the CSN by elaborating over the years progressive policy positions in the union's annual reports. In a series of papers, Pépin took responsibility for "A Society Made for Mankind"; "The Second Front"; "A Party of Freedom"; he then intensified his critique of Quebec's economic system with "There is no future for Quebec in the present economic system" and "Let's Rely Only on Our Own Means."[42] Meanwhile the FTQ, while maintaining a more moderate ideological stance, also advocated working class and popular solidarity. The publication of "L'Etat, rouage de notre exploitation" was characteristic of the FTQ's more radical position toward the Quebec state.

The increasingly critical postures assumed by both the CSN and the FTQ were linked to the unionization of public sector employees; to the ensuing confrontations with the state as the legislator of labour law and as employer; and to the worsening economic conditions within the province. This last factor tended to increase inter-union competition in most sectors, thus undermining labour solidarity. This was not, however, the case in the public and para-public sectors, where confrontations between the state and the union common front (CSN/FTQ/CEQ) assumed major proportions. For instance, in 1972, a general strike involving most public sector employees was organized by the common front. The Quebec government quickly passed back-to-work legislation to which the common-front leadership initially recommended disobedience. The front's leadership reconsidered their reaction and advised the membership to return to work. Some affiliates, among which were the hospital workers, refused to do so. In the meantime, the government had enacted a law prosecuting the union leaders for inciting civil disobedience. This led to further conflict between the provincial state and the union movement as some public buildings, and radio and television stations, were occupied by union members. At the same time, the politicization of the unions, through their manifestos and the political education of their members, led to a schism in the CSN and to the founding of the avowedly non-partisan Centrale des syndicats démocratiques (CSD) in 1972. By distancing itself from the radicalist elements of the unions and proposing a strategy of collaboration with business, the CSD sought to remain out of the political arena.

To a large extent the developments in organized labour in Quebec can be understood as a process of institutionalization similar to that which took place in the social science community. This is particularly true of the CSN. The attainment of a self-determining status for organized labour was a dual process: first the CSN had to free itself from the dominance of the church, while both the CSN and the FTQ had to free themselves from the dominance of the new intellectuals who succeeded the traditional elites. The growing independence of labour organizations from the middle-class intellectuals trained in the social sciences was reflected in the increasing distance of labour's political discourse from the dominant ideological discourse of *rattrapage* and technocratic "planning and participation," as well as in the through-the-ranks advancement of its organizational leaders. However, the ideological independence of labour from the new intellectuals was only partially attained by these developments. The unions' platform of participatory democracy required a fuller implementation of the planning and participation goals advocated by the statist intellectuals—not the presentation of a significantly different set of social goals.

Although the new intellectuals were removed from the leadership positions of organized labour, they did not disappear from the unions. Instead, they ultimately re-emerged as organizers and activists, and as workers in the educational and research branches of labour organizations. Roch Denis, Gilles Bourque, Jean-Marc Piotte, François Demers, and Raymond-G. Laliberté have occupied such roles. The production of analyses and manifestos couched in a Marxist conceptual framework, and internal union debates on the issues of the appropriate degree of political or partisan involvement and on the existence and role of political groups within the labour movement, owed much to their continuing influence. Thus, while the overt dominance of the intellectuals probably diminished as the 1960s unfolded, their actual influence as definers of the role and social goals of the unions persisted in new forms. This is all the more evident from the fact that the unions, even today, have not been able to elaborate a social platform that is not in some way dependent on the state–which since the Quiet Revolution has been, ideologically, the privileged terrain of the new middle class and its intellectual spokespersons.

Another concrete manifestation of social involvement is provided by *Parti pris*. Founded in 1963 by five young intellectuals, among whom were Pierre Maheu, Jean-Marc Piotte, Paul Chamberland, and André Brochu, students at the University of Montreal, and André Major, *Parti pris* was the main organ of the nationalist left until dissension among its editors and main contributors caused its disbandment in 1968. In the words of Roch Denis; "The journal, from its inception, [was] recognized for the radicalism of its positions in favour of socialism and the political independence of Quebec, and by its proclaimed breach with the generations of intellectuals whose position of 'objectivity' and of 'impartiality' left them as 'spectators of reality' rather than combatants in its transformation."[43] *Parti pris* adopted a Marxist definition of philosophy and science, which was reflected in its objectives. These were expressed in the following terms: "In relation to the goal of a free, secular and socialist Quebec state, the journal claims for itself the double function of 'demystifying' alienating structures and expressing, by reflecting and criticizing it, the revolution becoming conscious of itself as it proceeds."[44]

The journal's understanding of Quebec was based on a class analysis, in which the Quiet Revolution was defined in terms of the political and social success of a new industrial and (comparatively) progressive bourgeoisie dependent on the provincial state. Inspired by this analysis and by the social science literature on decolonization, its political position was one of tactical support for this ascendant class. The trade union movement was then seen as an obstacle to working-class consciousness because of its political moderation and its apparent support of *rattrapage*. The *Parti pris* manifesto of 1964–5 declared: "We are, in spite of ourselves, the objective allies of the national bourgeoisie in this first phase of the struggle; and we must sustain it and push it forward in its reformist enterprise."[45] One finds here an *étapiste* strategy, based on the view that independence must precede the building of a socialist society. According to this view, the transition period between the national democratic "revolution" (i.e., political sovereignty) and the socialist "revolution" would be characterized by the development of political cells and by popular education and mobilization.

With the slowing of the reforms of the Quiet Revolution, growing labour unrest, and the perception that the provincial government had abandoned its commitment to the social changes supported by the intellectual left, *Parti pris* reconsidered its position on the progressive character of the new national bourgeoisie. The *Mouvement Parti pris* (separate from the journal) was founded with the objective of developing a cadre of activists for an eventual party of the nationalist left. With the rediscovery of the working-class, this movement became the Mouvement de libération populaire (MLP) in 1965. The main theme and strategy of *Parti pris'* second manifesto (1965–6) was "the national democratic revolution under the impulse of the labouring classes."[46] It identified the labouring classes as those with an objective interest in the struggle for national independence and socialism. This second manifesto elaborated on the vanguard role of left-wing intellectuals, calling for the regrouping of leftist forces through the MLP and the development of a revolutionary party.

From 1966 until its demise in 1968, *Parti pris* experienced the typical problems and tribulations of the left. These centered not so much on the goals that should be pursued but on the question of the most effective strategy for attaining these ends without serious compromise or dilution. The divisions among the journal's contributors can be seen in the three, very different, strategic options defended in *Parti pris*. These were: (1) a workers' party linked to the trade unions; (2) a return to *étapisme* through support of the Rassemblement pour l'indépendance nationale (RIN) as the party of the progressive technocratic fraction of the new middle class; and (3) entry into the RIN in order to radicalize it and transform it into a workers' party. These differences on a practical course of action were also reflected in the journal's more theoretical perspective during its last several years, and by its adoption of a neutral position relative to the competing perspectives and representative organizations of the nationalist left. Like many other nationalist organizations, *Parti pris* was dealt a fatal blow by the founding in 1967 of the Mouvement souveraineté-association and then of the Parti Québécois; it disappeared from the scene in late 1968.

The case of *Parti pris* is a perfect example of the process in which one group of intellectuals attempts to replace its predecessor as the dominant ideological voice in society.[47] In the same way that social scientists of the late 1940s and 1950s had to discredit their predecessors in the academic, political, and social fields (a task that was largely centred around the critical journal *Cité libre*), those of the 1960s sought to disqualify theirs through the use of new frameworks of analysis and social involvement that established their relevance. The vanguardism of the *Parti pris* intellectuals, in a sense, replicated that of the *Cité-libristes*, but this time the object of criticism was not the power and the ideology of the traditional social order; rather, it was the Quiet Revolution itself, and the new middle class which had succeeded the traditional elites.

Ideological Fragmentation and the Demise of the Nationalist Consensus, 1970–1986

By the end of the 1960s an important division had emerged among Quebec social scientists. On one side were those who held positions within the provincial state: members of the technocratic middle class which had been at the same time a major force behind, and beneficiary of, the state expansion during the Quiet Revolution. They constituted the new clerisy, the ideological spokespersons for the nationalist new middle class, whose state-centred modernizing values had replaced the conservatism of the traditional elites as the dominant ideology in Quebec. On the other side were those who had become disillusioned with the pace of social reform, and with the provincial Liberal Party and the provincial state as vehicles for change. These critics of the new social order of the Quiet Revolution were associated with such socialist elements as the Rassemblement pour l'indépendance nationale (RIN), the Parti socialiste du Québec (PSQ), and the journal *Parti pris*. Despite ideological differences, most of the nationalist intellectual community threw its support behind the Parti Québécois in 1968. The PQ became the "official" party of national independence, temporarily ending the internecine squabbles over political strategies toward this goal.

There were, of course, those who did not share in this nationalist consensus, and who in fact advocated a federalist vision for Quebec. The entry into federal politics of two prominent *Cité-libristes*, Pierre Elliott Trudeau and Gérard Pelletier, together with the former head of the Confédération des syndicats nationaux (CSN), Jean Marchand, as well as the federalist commitment of such prominent Quebec intellectuals as the economist André Raynauld (who became chairman of the Economic Council of Canada), symbolized a different political option. The federalist option, however, did not enjoy wide favour, either among Quebec's francophone intellectuals as a whole, or among its social scientists as a group.

Several of those nationalist intellectuals were signatories to an open letter published in *Le Devoir* in reaction to Pierre Elliott Trudeau's speech of 30 November 1980 on the patriation of the Canadian Constitution.[1] Michèle Lalonde, Hélène Pelletier-Baillargeon, Paul Chamberland, and Denis Monière authored this letter. Marcel Rioux, Pierre Vadeboncoeur, Guy Rocher, Fernand Dumont, Yves Beauchemin, Gaston Miron, Gilles Vigneault, Michel Tremblay, and Jacques Grand'Maison were among those who signed, expressing their discontent with the nature of the constitutional initiative, if not their outright objection of the proposition itself.

With the electoral scene dominated be the Parti Québécois, socialist intellectuals turned to the universities, to activity in various urban social movements and municipal parties (e.g., FRAP), to research institutes (e.g., le Groupe de recherche interdisciplinaire en développement de l'Est du Québec; le Groupe de recherches sur l'espace, la dépendance et les inégalités; le Groupe de recherche et d'intervention régionales), and to the research departments of labour unions such as the CSN and the Centrale de l'enseignement du Québec (CEQ). Especially important was the creation of the Université du Québec system in 1968–9, with its mandate as an institution open to the participation of Quebec's "popular classes."[2] Université du Québec à Montréal became the seat of Québécois Marxist and socialist thinking. A new generation of social scientists, trained in France and weaned on the works of such Marxists as Nicos Poulantzas and Louis Althusser, came to dominate many departments in the social sciences. Their theoretical perspective led to new studies that re-examined Quebec society within the framework of class analysis.[3] Dominant themes were the existence or non-existence of an autonomous Quebec bourgeoisie and the role of the PQ in the transformation of Quebec's class structure. The political scientist Pierre Fournier and the sociologists Jorge Niosi and Gilles Bourque provided most of the ammunition for debate among the academic left. Fournier argued that one of the key political developments in Quebec since 1960 had been the emergence of a regional bourgeoisie with close ties to the Quebec state. Niosi, however, maintained that this francophone bourgeoisie was not necessarily regionally based; rather, it tended to be federalist in its political sympathies and actively opposed to the separation of Quebec from the rest of Canada. Bourque, whose writings were particularly influenced by the neo-Marxist literature, insisted that any understanding of Quebec society and social classes needed to be situated in its Canadian context.[4]

Whatever their theoretical value, the debates among Marxists about the most useful conceptual framework for understanding Quebec society in scientific-socialist terms became more and more esoteric and removed from practical affairs as the 1970s unfolded.[5] Thus, a leftist journal like

Les Cahiers du Socialisme had little to do with Lenin's classic question, "*Que faire?*"—"What is to be done?" Generally its writers were more concerned with the theoretical debates within a small coterie of university professors and Marxist intellectuals. Their isolation is not surprising, given the fact that no working-class party has ever successfully made its mark on Quebec's electoral scene. Faced with such political impotence, some Marxist intellectuals have remained outside both the mainstream party system and the universities and have assumed positions in urban social movements and in such independent institutes as the Centre de formation populaire (CFP), which seek to guide militant workers.

The Centre de formation populaire was created in 1971. In Marcel Fournier's words, it was part of "the movement of animation sociale which has existed in Quebec for the last ten years and which has mobilized many young intellectuals who have studied in the faculties of social sciences".[6] The CFP's objectives are "to become a crossroads for class exchanges, debates, and deepening of the diverse experiences of class struggle," and "to provide, while maintaining its autonomy, instruments and programs of education to activists of the workers' movement (trade unions, popular groups defending the interests of the workers, etc.)."[7] While the CFP is in the same tradition of political activism as *Parti pris*, it differs from that earlier forum for leftist intellectuals in that its membership includes popular organizations and the trade unions, not only individual activists. Thus, it is more a collective social intervention, as an organization for debates on class and for popular education, than a tentative ideological vanguard. The CFP's positions have reflected developments within its member organizations, including criticisms of Gomperist (i.e., non-class-conscious) trade unionism, co-operation with business, and petit-bourgeois nationalism, while advocating socialist independence and radical trade unionism. Furthermore, it has acted as a support group for the trade unions (especially the CSN and the CEQ) through its contribution to union education structures, political and social action committees, and the preparation and diffusion of their analyses and manifestos. The CFP also has organized education programs for workers on strike and has attempted to stimulate public debate on some of the class-related issues with which it is concerned. In 1973, the CFP expanded the range of its interventions and attempted to extend its programs of popular education to groups outside of the labour movement. To confirm its new mandate, the CFP prepared a manifesto that recognized its close association with the labour movement, emphasizing that it was not the mouthpiece of that movement. CFP objectives were such that it might act on behalf of labour but not at labour's behest; it would not limit its activities to union education. For the CFP, it was very important to maintain its independence by keeping at a certain distance from the unions.

Between 1974 and 1976, the CFP, (like *Parti pris* before it), encountered the proverbial divisions of the left. First, its claim to speak for the working class was cast in doubt by worker-intellectuals (i.e., intellectuals, working in factories, who denied the relevance of an organization of non-worker intellectuals linked to non-radical trade unions). Second, the CFP had to combat a Trotskyist group (linked to the journal *Mobilisation*) who attempted to take it over as an instrument of political class struggle. Since 1976, the CFP has managed to return to its 1973 manifesto and orientation, namely, maintaining close links with workers' organizations while preserving its independent position. Having established a certain distance from the labour movement, the CFP was in a position to reflect the ambivalence of the CSN and the CEQ by maintaining a "critical Yes" (the FTQ adopted a "Yes" position) leading up to the Referendum on sovereignty-association in May 1980. It characterized the Parti Québécois as a divided party, regrouping a neo-liberal tendency associated with part of the new middle class, and a social-democratic tendency associated with the segment of the new middle class centred on the provincial state.

The election of the PQ government in 1976 alleviated state-union tensions until after the May 1980 Referendum. This *rapprochement* was a result of the social-democratic stance of the PQ and of its efforts to gather support for its constitutional position. It need hardly be added that this honeymoon did not survive the government's defeat in the Referendum. In response to a difficult economic situation, the PQ government first came in conflict with its traditional ally, the technocratic middle class lodged in Quebec's public sector. In a series of labour laws, Bills 68, 70, 105, and 111, passed in 1982 and 1983, the government reduced pension benefits; dictated bargaining conditions and salaries; arbitrarily determined conditions of work for the next three years of public employees' contracts; and put an end to the CEGEP and public school teachers' strike, as well as imposed retroactive pay reductions in the public sector.[8]

The political impotence of the intellectual left has been aggravated by internal divisions. A sign of this disunity, and of the status of Quebec Marxist studies in general, has been the prevalence of foreign-inspired debates on the Quebec scene. Marcel Fournier complains that controversies imported from the French intelligentsia often gain ascendancy over issues more crucial and specific to Quebec society.[9] The rise and fall of the "structural Marxism" associated with the French Marxist Louis Althusser is telling in this regard. As the dominant tendency on the left in the early 1970s, Althusser's reading of Marx began to be questioned by those Quebec socialists who were inspired by the renegade critiques of Marxism made by Castoriadis and Lefebvre. In this connection, structural Marxism in Quebec has been attacked for what have been argued to be its implicit Leninist (some would say, Stalinist) tendencies toward a socialist totalitarianism. Demands for more decentralized forms of political organization in the struggle for socialism have become common. Perhaps this is testimony to the failure of nationalist politics at the provincial level to express socialist goals. The "third way" between capitalism and totalitarian communism has found numerous supporters in Quebec's leftist intelligentsia, many of whom now seek *"un socialisme autogestionnaire."*[10] The review *Possibles*, established in 1976 and informed by the issue of *autogestion*, constitutes an excellent example of this tendency. Its founding members included Marcel Fournier, Gabriel Gagnon, Gérald Godin, Gaston Miron, and Marcel Rioux. The share the goal of Quebec independence along with a vision of a decentralized socialist society.[11]

Inspired by this new intellectual direction, and by their perception that the field of economics needed to be made more relevant to Quebec society, a group of economics students met in Trois-Rivières in 1978 to form a political economy network. A journal, *Interventions critiques en économie politique*, was established to challenge the status quo accepted by mainstream economists. Influenced by new social movements, the editors decided in 1982 to give a social orientation to the journal; this was reflected in its new title, *Interventions économiques: Pour une alternative sociale.*

In fact, these "new" developments on the intellectual left recast values expressed in Quebec's long tradition of co-operative thought. Notwithstanding its imported Marxist elements, *autogestionnaire* thought has much to say about the declining status of farmers, disillusionment with the nationalist politics of the PQ, and the development of urban movements for participatory democracy. Together these constitute a receptive constellation of factors specific to Quebec. Illustrative of these developments is Serge Proulx' and Pierre Vallières' important publication, *Changer de société: Déclin du nationalisme, crise culturelle, alternatives sociales au Québec* (1982), which stresses Quebec's dynamic evolution.

Gilles Bourque and Jules Duchastel are pessimistic about these developments on the intellectual left. For them, the growth of *autogestionnaire* thought in Marxist circles, regardless of its intrinsic worth as a theory, is both a strategic blunder and an indication of the left's practical failure. They argue that such anti-statist theoretical stands play into the hands of the "new right" movements within Quebec, which seek non-interventionist policies for very different ideological reasons.

The ideological shift to the right among Quebec intellectuals is illustrated by the rising conservatism of l'Université du Québec à Montréal. Badly hit by budgetary cuts between 1976 and 1986, UQAM has evolved along lines rather different from those suggested by its original mandate. Instead of being open to all social classes as a training ground for progressive thinkers and social activists, UQAM *"se déplace vers la droite."* Bourque and Duchastel point to the rising age of professors, their increased profes-

Table 8

Total Full-Time Enrolment (All Levels) for Selected Fields at Univ. of Quebec
at Montreal

	1972–3	1975–6	1978–9	1981–2	1983–4
Fine Art	153	141	112	101	119
Philosophy	150	104	90	112	96
Commerce, Management, and Business Administration	253	465	1,108	2,832	3,995
Political Science	182	278	304	434	507
Social Work/Social Welfare	87	164	150	200	192
Sociology	124	309	282	362	392
Computer Science	–	42	–	403	722
Total enrolment (all fields)	4,727	6,367	7,295	11,295	13,402
Commerce, Management, and Business Administration as % of total	5.4	7.3	15.2	25.1	29.8

Source: Unpublished Statistics Canada data, special computation.

sionalism in union negotiations, and their willingness to bury the leftist
syndicalism, typical of the university in the early 1970s, as signs of the
taming of the left in Quebec. According to them, militant intellectuals
are much less likely to be found in the professorial circles at UQAM, or
in the CSN, CEQ, or CFP, but rather become active in fringe political
organizations and social movements. Consequently, UQAM has become
a more "utilitarian" university,[12] meeting the burgeoning demand for
courses in commerce and computer science. (See table 8.) Of course
UQAM has not been alone in facing pressure for change–pressure that
comes in part from the more conservative ideological and political orientations of Quebec's current generation of students.

Moreover, it is significant that the department of sociology at UQAM,
previously renowned for its neo-Marxist orientation, is leading the way
with an attempt at "depoliticizing" the social sciences. In 1982, Michel
Freitag, Gilles Bourque, Lizette Jalbert, and others founded the *Cahiers
de recherche sociologique*. In the words of its director, Michel Freitag, "The
creation of a series of research reports will contribute to the dynamic of
diversification and openness, whereby each current of analysis will come
to strengthen itself ... No single theory or particular *problématique* will
link together the various issues of this collection. Rather, the series is
satisfied to be unified by a common interest in society."[13] This trend
toward a more pluralistic approach also characterized the founding of

Politique by the Société québécoise de science politique in 1982. In the introduction to the journal Denis Monière stated: "This journal is going to reflect the political science that has developed in Quebec. It will be, therefore, pluralistic and accessible to various points of view."[14]

Despite the increasing diversity of theoretical and ideological approaches, the orientation of the social sciences continued to be primarily Quebec-centered. To some extent this bias was challenged by journals such as *Critère* (established by Jacques Dufresne in 1970) and *Sociologie et sociétés*, which tended to be more worldly in their focus. These professional developments point in the direction of greater ideological diversity in the social sciences, and a widely accepted right to express divergent viewpoints that reflect the "end of the national consensus" which, politically, had crystallized around the PQ in the 1970s. Quebec social scientists have distanced themselves from the political arena, a dégagement that may simply be a "hibernation,"[15] though it should be noted that they continue to be well represented in high government circles.

Although less passionate, perhaps, Quebec's social scientists remain very innovative and highly productive. Since the beginning of the 1980s—roughly coinciding with the decline of nationalism as a political issue—three intellectual trends have become prominent. The first trend situates Quebec within a Canadian perspective and reflects a major shift of emphasis among neo-Marxist intellectuals. Anne Legaré and Gilles Bourque began this line of interpretation in *Le Québec: La Question nationale* (1979). They were followed by several scholars, among whom were Gérard Boismenu in *Le Duplessisme* (1981), and Lizette Jalbert in *Régionalisme et luttes politiques: Une analyse des tiers partis au Canada et au Québec* (forthcoming). This new trend is also well represented in a recent collection of essays, *Espace régional et nation* (1983), to which Gérard Boismenu, Gilles Bourque, Roch Denis, Jules Duchastel, Lizette Jalbert, and Daniel Salée contributed. It is ironic that this group of scholars, who previously tended to emphasize Quebec's need for decolonization and self-assertion, now is proposing a Canadian model of interpretation.

The second trend involves a rediscovery of Quebec's regional problems, a renewed concern with uneven development within the province, and a realization of the significance of regional popular movements. Several social scientists have concentrated their recent efforts on examining Quebec's regions and proposing new avenues for development. Fernard Harvey (Institut québécois de recherche sur la culture), Clermont Dugas, Hughes Dionne, and Bruno Jean (Université du Québec à Rimouski), Jean-Jacques Simard (Université Laval), Juan Luis Klein (Université du Québec à Chicoutimi), and Alain G. Gagnon (Carleton University), among others, are working within this stream. Both the Groupe de recherche interdisciplinaire en développement de l'Est du Québec (GRI-

DEQ), established in 1975, and the Institut québécois de recherche sur la culture (IQRC), established in 1979 under the directorship of Fernand Dumont, have provided much of the needed institutional and financial support for this second research trend.

In a third trend, Quebec social scientists have come to realize the diversity of their society. Leading the way once more in institutional support is the IQRC. This highly intellectual centre for research has sponsored several studies pertaining to Quebec's ethno-cultural communities: *The English of Québec: From Majority to Minority Status* (1982); *La communauté grecque du Québec* (1983); *Les Etudes ethniques au Québec* (1983); *Juifs et réalités juives au Québec* (1984); and *The Forgotten Quebecers: A History of English-speaking Québec, 1759-1980* (1985).

The metamorphosis of UQAM, from a hotbed of academic Marxism to a more conservative institution in which the popularity of the social sciences has waned while that of business-related disciplines has risen, has already been discussed. Developments at UQAM, however, are not unique, but reflect a more general transformation of higher education institutions in Quebec. This transformation is largely a result of changes in the relationship of Quebec's new middle classes to the provincial state. Due to the fiscal crisis of the Quebec state and the relative youth of those currently employed in the public and para-public sectors, the sons and daughters of the new middle class are unable to follow the career patterns of their parents. In addition, the success of the provincial government's linguistic policies has opened new opportunities for the middle classes in the private sector.[16]

Gilles Paquet, dean of the Faculty of Administration at the University of Ottawa, shares this view, and maintains that Bill 101 completed the transformation necessary for the consolidation of a Quebec business class: "By triggering an important emigration of anglophones and discouraging the immigration of young anglophones from the rest of the country, important opportunities were created for a generation of young, well-educated and experienced Québécois."[17]

The PQ's rejection of the independence option in January 1985, eight years after its initial ascent to power, symbolized the new era in Quebec politics. Economic problems and the role of the state in furthering Quebec's position in world markets now dominate policy papers and seminars. On 23 September and 7 October 1983, Camille Laurin organized two conferences which brought together eighty members of Quebec's nationalist intelligentsia. The communiqué from these conferences included criticisms of the PQ, as a *dirigiste* and centralist party increasingly out of touch with the general population (*le nous*). An ideological shift away from state nationalism to neo-liberalism is quite evident in one of the slogans proclaimed in the communiqué: "La prise en main personnelle précède la prise en main nationale." (Before we worry about the self-reliance of the nation we must worry about the self-reliance of the individual.)[18]

Thomas J. Courchene speaks of a fundamental ideological transformation, which he calls "market nationalism." He argues: "Although the state still has an important place in terms of the new political economy, its role now is really to facilitate Québécois capitalism ... Quebecers are not merely trying to better themselves economically: they are taking a quantum gamble that they can quickly make the transition from transfer dependency to economic independence and that they are counting on the market or market-oriented processes to accomplish this goal."[19] The policy agenda of the 1970s and early 1980s, which included a heavy stress on constitutional reform, linguistic protectionism and social policy, is being replaced by the issues of deregulation, the privatization of state assets and ways to increase the competitiveness of the provincial economy.[20]

The election of Robert Bourassa's Liberals in December 1985 confirmed this *virage*, as three government-appointed task forces on deregulation (Reed Scowen), state reorganization (Paul Gobeil), and privatization (Pierre Fortier) were set up. These task forces were all business-dominated as, for example, the presence of Michel Bélanger (president of the National Bank), Pierre Lortie (president of Provigo), and Yvon Marcoux (former vice-president of the Banque d'épargne, later appointed president of the Société générale de financement) on the Gobeil task force, clearly revealed.[21]

As Richard French has observed, "the hegemony of Quebec's technocrats, nationalist social scientists, and literary intelligentsia is quickly being eroded by the rise of a new *bourgeoisie d'affaires*."[22] This new bourgeoisie represents Quebec's own version of the more general phenomenon of the young urban professionals ("Yuppies"). "Social leadership, held for a decade by an intellectual bourgeoisie and those in the field of communication, is rapidly shifting to the business or economic bourgeoisie ... It remains to be seen which of these will have power in Quebec: those who define political discourse with the government and whose ultimate objective is independence, or those whose preoccupations are economic and thus oriented toward investment and expansion of the Quebec market."[23] The return of the Quebec Liberal Party to power suggests a realignment of class forces favouring the business community,[24] or what Alain G. Gagnon and Khayyam Z. Paltiel refer to as a "Balzacian bourgeoisie."[25] The role of the provincial state has been shifted toward the interests of a community whose commitment to nationalist goals has always been limited, at best.

The current crisis of nationalism can also be understood as a crisis of interventionism, in which the legitimacy of the *dirigiste* élite and its social-democratic and statist rhetoric have been called into question. Supplanting this *étatisme* is a neo-liberal rhetoric which generally demands less state intervention, but at the same time seeks government policies that support the domestic and international competitiveness of Quebec firms.

Evidence of the ideological shift that Quebec has undergone since the disintegration of the nationalist consensus is plentiful. Perhaps most revealing is the relative decline in the popularity, among university students, of the social sciences compared to business-related programs. Before the Quiet Revolution the avenues for upward socio-economic mobility were mainly within the liberal professions. As the former PQ finance minister Jacques Parizeau has put it, "For a long time in Quebec, if you had good marks in school, you went into medicine, law or the priesthood. If you didn't do so well you went into business or whatever."[26] These career patterns for the aspiring middle class reinforced the traditional social order by failing to generate alternative francophone elites. This situation changed with the expansion of the Quebec state in the 1960s and the secularization of the rapidly growing para-public sector. A university education in the social sciences acquired both a social prestige and a market value that it had not previously possessed, and this was reflected in increasing university enrolment in social science programs. But times have changed again. In 1983–4, the fields of commerce, management, and business administration accounted for half of the total Bachelor's degree enrolment in the social sciences (see table 9). Enrolment in these fields, as a percentage of total enrolment, has almost doubled since 1972. While new undergraduate programs have been created and existing programs expanded, Master's programs in commerce, management and business administration have grown only enough to preserve their share of the enrolled population.

The increasing popularity of business administration among university students in Quebec is a revealing indication of the shift since the 1960s in the ideological climate of that province. As a vocationally oriented discipline, by its very nature concerned with imparting the knowledge and skills necessary for successful behavior within a capitalist economic system, business administration is inherently supportive of the social institutions that accompany the capitalist economy. Moreover, it is not a "pure" social science like economics, sociology, or political science (though it too studies human behavior), being a borrower of concepts developed in sociology, social psychology, microeconomics, and systems theory.

Another important tendency which demonstrates the dimensions of the growth of business-oriented education in francophone Quebec has been the increasing enrolment of francophones in English-language in-stitutions. While available data is limited, figures for Bishop's and McGill Universities show that the percentage of francophones enrolled in business

Table 9

Bachelor's Degree Enrolment in the Social Sciences in Quebec, by Discipline, 1983–1984

	No.	% of social sciences
Commerce/Management/Business Administration	14,101	50.7
Law	2,842	10.2
Psychology	2,362	8.5
Economics	2,254	8.1
Political Science	1,716	6.2
Social Work	1,057	3.8
Sociology	992	3.6
Geography	883.	3.2
Others	1,631	5.9
Total Social Sciences	27,838	100%

Source: Statistics Canada, Universities: enrolment and degrees, 1983.

programs at these universities almost doubled between 1972–3 and 1983–4. More than 20 per cent of the students enrolled at the three existing English-language institutions (Bishop's, McGill, Concordia) in 1983–4 were francophones, while the number of anglophones in the French-language institutions has remained negligible. The growing popularity of business education among francophones in Quebec has indeed been dramatic, surpassing even the national trend.[27]

The "business revolution" cannot pass without comment. It is simply too dramatic a change in a province where for so long a classical education and entry into the liberal professions were the paths to elite status. Indeed, these educational and professional backgrounds continue to be common among the older generation of Quebec's political and bureaucratic elites. At present, Quebec's six major business schools are graduating more than 400 MBAs a year with approximately 250 from McGill, and the remainder from the Ecole des Hautes études commerciales (HEC), UQAM, Concordia, Sherbrooke, and Laval.[28] Moreover, the HEC claims 8,000 students at both undergraduate and graduate levels, which makes it the largest business school in Canada, outnumbering its closest rival, York University's school of business and administration.[29]

To a large extent, journals of social criticism such as *Cité libre*, *Parti pris*, and *La Vie en rose*, have been displaced by journals with an economic orientation. Among these latter are *Finance*, *L'Analyste*, and *Le Devoir*

Table 10
Occupational Distribution of Quebec Cabinet Ministers, 1976–1987 (percentages)

Occupation	Lévesque/Johnson 1976–85	Bourassa 1985–
Agriculture	1.9	–
Business, public administration, entrepreneurs	20.4	38.4
Law	20.4	26.9
Education	25.9	11.5
Journalism	9.3	3.8
Medicine	5.5	–
Engineering	1.9	7.7
Other	14.7	11.5

Source: Gouvernement du Québec, *Répertoire des parlementaires québécois, 1867–1978* (Québec: Assemblée Nationale du Québec 1980); *Canadian Parliamentary Guide*, selected years; selected issues of *Le Devoir* and *La Presse*. This table is based on a subjective assessment of profession. One half point was given if two careers were pursued (i.e., one half for each). Political careers were not included in the calculation.

économique. A business-oriented newspaper, *Les Affaires*, has tripled its circulation during the last five years, reaching 100,000 copies in 1987.

The erstwhile growth of the social sciences has now ended, and the new form of "intellectual capital" being produced is oriented more towards private enterprise functions than state planning.[30] The discrediting of statism and nationalism has been accompanied by changes in the education and career choices of the middle classes in Quebec, and thus in the objective interests of the new generation currently being educated for jobs in the private sector. From the standpoint of the dominant ideology and its spokespersons, this means that Camille Laurin, Marcel Léger, Gérald Godin, Jacques Parizeau, and René Lévesque are "out" and Pierre Fortier, Pierre Macdonald, Paul Gobeil, and Robert Bourassa are "in."

The composition of the Bourassa cabinet reflects this change of guard. The number of ministers with business, public administration, and finance backgrounds in 1985–6 amounted to 38.4 per cent, compared to an average of 20.4 per cent during the PQ administrations. In contrast, 35.2 per cent of cabinet ministers during the period of 1976–85 had a background in education and journalism compared to 15.3 per cent in the present Bourassa cabinet.

The particularly high proportion of teachers in the Quebec National Assembly cannot pass unnoticed. According to Maurice Pinard, the presence of teachers and professors has been quite in evidence in the formation of PQ cabinets, as intellectuals, to a large extent, assumed dominance of Quebec politics between 1976 and 1985.

Table 11

"République des professeurs," Selected Years

	% Intellectuals (all types)	% Teachers and Professors
Quebec Labour Force (1981)	7	5
Among francophone Yes Voters (1980)	11	n.a.
Among PQ Members (1979)	n.a.	16
Among PQ Convention delegates (1969)	n.a.	22[a]
Among PQ Convention delegates (1981)	n.a.	24
Among PQ Executive members (1968–77)	n.a.	36
Among PQ Candidates (1976)	53	44
Among PQ Deputies (1981)	51	44
Among PQ Cabinet ministers (1979)	62	54

Source: Maurice Pinard and Richard Hamilton, "The Leadership Roles of Intellectuals in Party Politics," unpublished paper, 1987.

[a] Data provided in Gérard Bergeron, Notre miroir à deux faces (Montréal: Québec/Amérique 1985), 126.

With the return of Bourassa's Liberals to power in 1985, the presence of teachers diminished so substantially that they no longer constitute the dominant group in Quebec party politics. Moreover, a number of prominent public servants have decided to join the business revolution. Among them are Michel Bélanger, Claude Castonguay, André Saumier, and Raymond Garneau. Once senior bureaucrats in Quebec City, they respectively went on to preside over the National Bank, La Corporation La Laurentienne (the third largest financial holding company in Canada), the Montreal Stock Exchange (Saumier resigned in 1987), and the Montreal and District Savings Bank (Garneau returned to politics at the 1984 federal election).

Only the future, however, will tell whether Quebec's newly emerging business class will be able to overcome such economic problems as the deindustrialization of Montreal, its decline as a commercial centre, and the province's dependence on tariff–protected and declining industries, thereby justifying the abandonment of the goals of the Quiet Revolution. If not, the disappointed expectations of the younger generation of Québécois being trained for places in the business world may prove a force that can be mobilized behind a resurgent nationalism focused on the role of the provincial state.

The Quebec government is very keen to indicate that it wishes to consolidate its links with the business class. Premier Bourassa is quoted as saying that "The presence of strong, dynamic and well-entrenched Quebec enterprises means that economic power will stay in Quebec hands. But instead of resting with the state, it will be in the hands of Quebec businessmen."[31]

The recommendations of the Gobeil Report point in the direction of a weakening of the social sciences. In an attempt to reduce government spending, it has proposed that several research centres be abolished: the Institut national de productivité; the Institut de recherche en santé et en sécurité du travail; and the Institut québécois de recherche sur la culture (IQRC).[32] The priorities of the Quebec government no longer include significant support for the social sciences in Quebec. Instead, the priorities are deregulation, privatization, and state reorganization. This agenda reflects the fact that a new clerisy has come to dominate Quebec politics. This new clerisy, structured around the fields of economics, public administration, management, and business, is replacing the one which emerged in the 1960s and 1970s, formed of poets, journalists, sociologists, and political scientists.

To conclude this chapter on a speculative note, one might ask whether the *dégagement* of Quebec intellectuals characteristic of the post-referendum period will last, or whether it will give way to a renewed politicization. Changes noted earlier in the focus and theoretical orientation of academic work suggest the emergence of a new era in Quebec politics, a period of ideological pluralism. Claude Martin and Marc-Henry Soulet explain *l'hiver québécois des sociologues*; the "winter" of political *dégagement* and the greater intellectual pluralism that currently characterizes Quebec's social science community, as follows: "No longer having truly the activist vision since the disappearance of the nationalist hope, they no longer feel themselves to be bearers of the collective vision. Besides, collaboration with the péquiste version of the administrative state has led to too many compromises for this role to be considered viable, Thus, they have rediscovered the virtues and the comfort of withdrawal and of the qualified statement."[33] It remains to be seen whether their abandonment of the historic function of educated elites in Quebec—namely, to express the "collective vision," as in the "Oui des écrivains"[34] of the 1980 Referendum campaign—represents more than a temporary hibernation.

PART TWO

English Canada

CHAPTER FOUR

The Clerisy of Social Scientists, 1945–1963

It would probably be difficult to find another modern
political system with such a paucity of participation
from its scholars. In almost all countries of the western
world scholars work close to political parties and even
take on important political roles. The absence of any
dynamic quality to the Canadian political system could
probably in a large measure be attributed to its
separation from the world of higher learning.

John Porter, *The Vertical Mosaic*

While much has been written on the social sciences in English Canada
from the standpoint of their expansion and intellectual development,
their political significance rarely has been considered. Exceptions include
various assessments by C.B. Macpherson,[1] and a relatively brief discussion
by John Porter, in *The Vertical Mosaic*,[2] of the ideological function of the
social sciences. More recently, a number of sociologists have examined
the phenomenon of increasing nationalism within the Canadian social
science community and have attributed this to what they argue are the
class stresses engendered by Canada's dependent economic structure.[3]
But generally it is the case that, aside from historical and biographical
material containing scattered insights into the role played by particular
individuals in the policy process, there has been very little consideration
of the *collective* significance of social science intellectuals.[4]

John Porter's statement suggests that one ought not to be surprised
at the lack of reflection on the political significance of social scientists
in Canada—in view of the fact that there has been so little to reflect on.
But, as Porter himself recognized in his use of the concept "clerisy" to
describe the higher education establishment, the English-Canadian intellectual elite has exercised a political function through its uncritical
acceptance of the principal features of the social order. Acquiescence is

every bit as "ideological" as dissent; it differs only in terms of its relationship to the status quo. And certainly the period in the intellectual history of English Canada that Porter was reflecting on was not remarkable for social criticism. Porter's assessment of the relationship of Canadian intellectuals to the social order was categorical: "Judged by the internal standards of their function within Canadian social institutions, the universities and their leading teachers can be said to be appropriate to other institutional aspects of Canadian society. Upward social mobility is limited, the British charter group dominates, the political system is depoliticized in a crippling federalism. Over all this ruminate the disengaged fellows of the Royal Society of Canada, Section II."[5]

Porter does not attempt to explain the conservative disposition of the intellectual elite in English Canada; this is not central to his task of describing the structure of inequality reflected in the institutions of Canadian society. The beginnings of such an explanation are provided by C. B. Macpherson. In his 1957 assessment of the state of the social sciences in Canada, he identifies the main themes that have informed social thought and history in French and English Canada. Macpherson makes several suggestive observations regarding the political significance the social sciences. Briefly, he argues that the development of the social sciences was heavily conditioned by the same forces that have shaped Canada's economic development: thus, intellectual life in English Canada had been colonized, first by Britain, and then by the United States. However, Canadian society could not adequately be understood with only imported techniques and frameworks of analysis. A distinctive Canadian mode of analysis emerged: this was the political economy of Harold Innis, Vernon Fowke, W. A. Mackintosh, and others.[6] Macpherson goes beyond a historiography of the social sciences to argue that social scientists, and particularly historians, inevitably convey political values in their interpretations of society. Indeed, he goes so far as to refer to French Canadian historians as "intellectual patriots" in the service of *la nation*. Of their English Canadian counterpart Macpherson writes, "He may have a political faith, but it does not dominate his history."[7] (It should be noted that the French-Canadian historian Michel Brunet, writing two years later, argued that romantic and functionally ideological interpretations of history were no less common in English than in French Canada.)[8]

As in the case of Quebec, particular schools were influential in shaping the relationship of social scientists to politics in English Canada. Indeed, it is reasonable to speak of two very different traditions associated with, respectively, Queen's University and the University of Toronto. Queen's has had a long history of producing graduates for the Ottawa bureaucracy; the University of Toronto did not have a comparable tradition of public service. Individual exceptions to this generalization are not difficult to find, but the distinction stands. With the proliferation and growth of social science faculties at other universities (perhaps more importantly, with the passing of the Ottawa mandarinate of the 1940s and 1950s),[9] the distinctive relationship of Queen's to the federal state has disappeared.

The Queen's connection with the federal government predates the period of this study by several decades beginning at a time when the intellectual and professional barriers between economists, political scientists, and historians were low. The economic historian Adam Shortt held various official positions with both the federal and Ontario governments and from 1908 to 1917 was one of the two members of the Civil Service Commission of Canada. Shortt was an original member of the Canadian Political Science Association (CPSA). His views on the purpose of that organization reflected the tradition of practical scholarship of which he was an exemplar: "One does not attempt fine work through the instrumentality of a mob ... It is through a select, active minority that the most effective and progressive ideas as to political and social welfare must be introduced."[10] The CPSA was intended to be an agency for the expert analysis of political problems, being comprised of academics and members of the political and bureaucratic elites.

In 1908 Shortt was succeeded as Sir John A. Macdonald Professor of Political and Economic Science at Queen's by Oscar Douglas Skelton, formerly a student of political science at the University of Chicago. Skelton's scholarship, like Shortt's, was heavily influenced by his interest in contemporary economic and social issues. Moreover, his commitment to liberalism and capitalism constituted a further similarity to Shortt— both of them being dedicated to the *solution* of problems within liberal capitalism rather than criticism of its fundamental premises. Indeed, it is part of the lore of Canadian intellectual history that Skelton's *Socialism: A Critical Appraisal* (1911) received the distinction of being referred to by Lenin as a sophisticated embodiment of intellectual power in the service of capitalism. Skelton's insistence that Canadian foreign policy should be determined independently of the British empire, and that Canada's most important external relationship was with the United States, coincided with the views of the Liberal Prime Minister, Mackenzie King. In 1925 Skelton was appointed by King as Under-Secretary of State for External Affairs, and until his death in 1941 was beyond doubt the most influential figure in Canada's foreign policy—an influence acknowledged by King in several passages from his diaries.[11] Indeed, J.L. Granatstein dates the beginning of the modern civil service in Canada from Skelton's entry into the Ottawa bureaucracy. Skelton recruited into External Affairs several highly educated individuals, many of whom had done their postgraduate work at Oxford and had a broad general education in line with the British notion of suitable training for high-ranking civil servants. Among those recruited were Lester Pearson, Norman Robertson, and Hugh Keenleyside, all of whom had received their graduate training in history. In addition, Skelton was the director of research for the Royal Commission on Dominion-Provincial Relations (1937).

Another professor from Queen's, the economist W.C. Clark, was appointed in 1932 as Deputy Minister of Finance. Clark's role as one of the key architects of Keynesian economic policy after World War II is widely acknowledged. He was at the centre of a group of Queen's economists who were prominent members of the bureaucratic elite through their positions in the Department of Finance and the Bank of Canada. This group included W.A. Mackintosh and John Deutsch, each of whom served as Deputy Minister of Finance and ultimately became Principal of Queen's. Below the level of the Ottawa mandarinate of this period, Queen's developed a reputation as a recruiting ground for the federal bureaucracy.

By comparison, not one of the individuals described by John Porter as "Dr. Clark's boys" was recruited from the faculty of the University of Toronto. Under the influence of Harold Adams Innis, the Department of Political Economy at Toronto remained comparatively detached from the political process. Innis's style of scholarship involved communicating with other academics rather than taking part in contemporary debates and attempting to mobilize support for some position on an issue. His biographer, the historian Donald Creighton, writes that Innis was contemptuous of political parties, and of the academics associated with the League for Social Reconstruction.[12] At precisely the time when the circumstances of the Depression and the outbreak of World War II contributed to increased pressure on social scientists to direct their energies toward the solution of contemporary problems, Innis insisted on scholarly detachment. Carl Berger writes: "Innis stood against the rising tide of demands on scholars to participate more directly in the political life of the country. He was critical of the LSR and the case for centralization of the Rowell-Sirois Report, and he came to see the participation of academics in radical politics, or even their joining the state bureaucracy, as disastrous threats to Canadian scholarship."[13] Despite his criticism of academic participation in the Rowell-Sirois Commission (including his charge that the special studies carried out by economists were merely window-dressing for a policy agenda that Ottawa's governing elite had already decided upon),[14] Innis himself was not above participating in the non-partisan side of politics on an occasional basis. This was demonstrated by his work for the Nova Scotia Royal Commission on the Economy (1934) and his membership on the federal Royal Commission on Transportation (1948–51). However, under his leadership the social

Table 12

Political Science Publications in the *Canadian Journal of Economics and Political Science* by General Subject, 1945–1964

	1945–54		1955–64	
	No.	%	No.	%
1) Institutions and Public Administration	53[a]	31.7	37[c]	21.8
2) Political Philosophy, Ideology, and Theory	28	16.8	28	16.5
3) Parliamentary Process, Representation, and Cabinet	18	10.8	14	8.2
4) Political Parties, Elections, and Social Movements	19	11.4	22	12.9
5) Public Policy	18	10.8	16	9.4
6) Socio-economic Class	2	1.2	11[d]	6.5
7) Other	29[b]	17.4	42[e]	24.7
Total	167	100.1[f]	170	100.0

Note: Each work has been assigned to a single subject category. Although many articles relate to two or more categories, in only a small number of cases was it difficult to identify a dominant theme. For example, we assigned C.B. Macpherson's "M,arket Concepts in Political Theory" to (2), not (6); Rudolf Heberle's "Parliamentary Government and Political Parties" to (3), not (4); and Hugh G. Thorburn's "Parliament and Policy-Making: The Case of the Trans-Canada Gas Pipeline" to (5), not (3). The resident category "Other" includes works on social cleavages, historical events and figures, some comparative studies, works on methodology, international relations, and articles on the state of the discipline.

[a] This category includes nine published works specifically on the constitution, and one on UN sanctions.

[b] Nine of these works, or 31 per cent of this category, were on subjects relating to social cleavages. For example: K.D. Naegele, "Hostility and Aggression in Middle-Class American Families"; Jean-C. Falardeau, "The Parish as an Institutional Type"; and S.D. Clark, "The Religious Sect in Canadian Economic Development."

[c] This category includes eight works specifically on the constitution.

[d] Five of these works were written by John Porter, and a sixth was a direct comment on one of his articles.

[e] Fourteen of these works, or 33.3 per cent of this set, were on subjects relating to social cleavages.

[f] Percentages do not add up to 100.0 due to rounding error.

sciences at the University of Toronto, unlike the tradition at Queen's, were not oriented towards the needs of the state.

One of the outstanding features of scholarship in the social sciences during the period up to the early 1960s is that the concept of class is so rarely employed.[15] The images conveyed by social scientists included motifs of conflict, but these involved conflict between ethnolinguistic or religious groups, between regional economies, or between governments. A survey of articles, notes, memoranda, and reviews published in the

Canadian Journal of Economics and Political Science (CJEPS) between 1945 and 1964 provides some indication of the subjects that concerned this group of Canadian social scientists.

While a range of subjects is reflected in CJEPS during this period, studies of institutions, the constitution, and administrative structures and processes account for roughly a quarter of the contributions. At the other extreme, works which have as their central theme socio-economic class (defined broadly to include studies on elites, power and inequality), constitute only a handful of all published works. Over half of the increase in this category between 1945–54 and 1955–64 is attributable to John Porter's various articles. The number of works in the residual category increased significantly in these two decades, due to increases in the number of comparative studies, pieces on methodology, and work on social cleavages.

This impression of a discipline that was reinforcing the image of Canada as a society in which class divisions were of little consequence is corroborated in Donald Smiley's review of major publications in Canadian political science during the post-war period. He suggests that the discipline moved from the institutionalist approach epitomized in R. Macgregor Dawson's *The Government of Canada*,[16] to the behaviorist concern with individuals and groups in politics (the "input" side of the political system), with various broad interpretive works scattered across the landscape. Smiley identifies John Porter's *The Vertical Mosaic* (1965) as a turning point in Canadian social science: "The most important part of Porter's analysis for students of Canadian politics is his focus on class analysis both as an explanatory factor and as a source of norms by which to evaluate the political system. In doing so, he challenges most of the prevailing intellectual currents. There is here a rejection of the contemporary emphasis on cultural duality ... (and away) from the traditional preoccupation of Canadian scholars with nation-building and national unity."[17]

If political scientists in Canada were not challenging conventional conceptions of Canadian society through their published work (and one assumes that what was imparted in the classroom could not have been significantly different), one might reasonably ask why this was so. Part of the answer lies in the relatively underdeveloped state of political science, and of the social sciences generally, in Canada at this time. It has been estimated that there were no more than thirty full-time professors of political science in the mid-1950s; it is certainly the case that a single department, the Department of Political Economy at the University of Toronto, dominated the discipline. Between 1950 and 1960 the corps of political scientists and other social scientists grew in response to increased undergraduate enrolments, but continued to draw on graduates of major universities in the United States and the United Kingdom. This pattern of dependent development continued through the expansionary period of the 1960s as the shortfall between the teaching needs of social science departments and the number of qualified individuals trained in Canadian graduate programs was acute. Table 13 illustrates this fact.

Thus, at the beginning of the 1960s the social science community in Canada was small, overwhelmingly trained elsewhere, and based primarily in the universities. This last feature was less characteristic of economics than of political science and sociology, as increasing numbers of economists entered the employ of the state. Precise figures are scarce; but in 1967 a former Deputy Minister of Finance, R.B. Bryce, estimated that 220 professional economists (i.e., individuals holding master's or doctor's degrees in economics) were employed in the public service.[18] Figures provided by Anthony Scott suggest that by the early 1960s the ratio of university-employed to state-employed economists was 60:40.[19] Comparable estimates for political scientists and sociologists are not available, but it is doubtful that state employment levels approached that of their economics colleagues, since as the scope of state intervention in the economy increased, the demand for professional economists also grew. Consequently, whereas political science and sociology were oriented primarily toward the university between 1945 and 1965, economics was divided between the university and the state. This difference is corroborated by data on the appointment of PHD graduates to positions in the federal bureaucracy between 1940 and 1972, as shown in table 14.

The links between the federal bureaucracy and the university during this period have been examined by John Porter. He found that in 1953 just under a fifth of the bureaucratic elite (comprised of the 243 senior officials of federal government departments, agencies and crown corporations) had taught in a university at some point, and an even greater proportion of the highest ranking bureaucrats (nine out of forty individuals at the deputy-ministerial level)[20] were former university teachers. Prominent among those whose careers spanned the intellectual and bureaucratic elites were such economists as W.C. Clark, R.B. Bryce, W.A. Mackintosh, and John Deutsch. The unrivalled dominance of the Department of Finance in economic policy and (to the extent that there were financial implications) in social policy as well, meant that this group, and the economics profession generally, had a relationship to public policy not enjoyed by other social scientists. This was evident in the formation and activities of the Royal Commission on Canada's Economic Prospects (the Gordon Commission), which issued its preliminary report in 1956. In the words of a writer for the *Canadian Forum*, "The Gordon Commission was like a vast wind tunnel with the door accidentally left open: it sucked up practically every available economist in the country."[21]

Table 13

Full-time University Teachers and the Number of Doctoral Degrees Awarded
in Canada by Discipline, 1960–1961 to 1971–1972

Discipline	No. of Teachers	No. of Doctorates Awarded
Economics[a]		
1960–1	216	10
1961–2	244	5
1962–3	272	6
1963–4	312	7
1964–5	567	12
1965–6	423	14
1966–7	508	10
1967–8	594	20
1968–9	679	21
1969–1970	762	15
1970–1	766	28
1971–2	860	27
Political Science[b]		
1960–1	54	2
1961–2	73	1
1962–3	93	2
1963–4	123	2
1964–5	162	–
1965–6	200	5
1966–7	264	1
1967–8	328	10
1968–8	385	8
1969–1970	450	18
1970–1	561	21
1971–2	684	31
Sociology		
1960–1	61	
1961–2	72	
1962–3	84	
1963–4	115	
1964–5	155	
1965–6	195	
1966–7	248	

Table 13 (continued)

Discipline	No. of Teachers	No. of Doctorates Awarded
1967–8	300	
1968–9	410	
1969–1970	548	
1970–1	702	
1971–2	829	

Source: Adapted from Statistics Canada, *University Education Growth, 1960–61 to 1971–72* (Catalogue 81-559), 94, table 45; and Max von Zur-Muehlen, *The Full-Time Faculty of Canadian Universities, 1956–57 to 1974–75* (Statistics Canada, Institutional and Public Finance Branch, 15 April 1977), 36, table 14.

ᵃ This category includes doctorates granted in commerce and business.
ᵇ This category includes doctorates granted in sociology.

The special relationship of economics to public policy in Canada had begun to take shape in the 1930s. The recruitment of university-trained economists for the Department of Finance and the research department of the newly created (1935) Bank of Canada, as well as for the economic studies commissioned for the Nova Scotia Royal Commission on the Economy (1934), the National Employment Commission (1936), and the Royal Commission on Dominion-Provincial Relations (1937–40), provided the institutional opportunities for the increasing integration of the economics profession into the state. In terms of intellectual developments, it is clear that even before Keynes's ideas on the manipulation of aggregate demand by government became the orthodox view, there existed widespread skepticism about the self-correcting markets of classical economic theory. The financial collapse of 1929 and the ensuing Depression reinforced these doubts and created a climate of receptivity for the alternative theory that was set forth in *The General Theory of Employment, Interest and Money* (1936).[22]

World War II saw state planning on a level never previously experienced in Canada, with increasing recruitment of university economists into such government bodies as the Department of Finance and the Wartime Prices and Trade Board. They formed the core of what Mackenzie King refered to as the "intelligentsia": a group of experts for whom wartime planning provided opportunities to influence policy from *within* the state.[23] Their influence, and the special relationship of the economics profession to public policy, was consolidated by the government's formal acceptance of Keynesian economic policy, in the White Paper on *Employment and Income* (12 April 1945) and in the Liberal Party's 1945 election platform. Keynesianism represented not simply a shift in the dominant model within the economics discipline but also produced a new conception of the economist's role in a capitalist society. Previously, the practitioners

Table 14

Appointment of PHD Graduates to Federal Departments under the Public Service
Employment Act,[a] by Discipline and Year of Appointment

	Economics	Political Science	Sociology and Anthropology
1940–9	3	2	1
1950–4	10	3	–
1954–9	11	3	1
1960	2	1	2
1961	3	–	1
1962	3	1	–
1963	1	–	1
1964	4	1	1
1965	3	1	1
1966	2	3	1
1967	8	1	3
1968	10	1	2
1969	4	2	2
1970	14	1	4
1971	15	–	2
1972	11	–	2
Total	104	21	25

Source: Adapted from Max von Zur-Muehlen, The Ph.D. Dilemma in Canada Revisited (Statistics Canada, Institutional and Public Finance Branch, 1 May 1977), 20, table 8.

[a] Excludes the National Research Council, the Defense Research Board, and all crown corporations.

of the "dismal science" were inclined to take the view that government interference with cyclical fluctuations in the economy was likely to aggravate what was understood to be temporary disequilibrium in the marketplace. The ideological role of the classical economist was to preach the virtues of the *laissez-faire* state, in which the legitimate government policy was to control monopolistic tendencies within the economy. The Keynesian doctrine, however, assigned an economic management role to government, requiring experts whose job it would be to assemble and analyze the data required for counter-cyclical economic policy. Moreover, as a major dimension of Keynesian economic management was the manipulation of consumer spending, the emerging social welfare state could be harnessed for purposes of economic policy. Indeed, it appears that the impetus behind one of the earliest planks of Canada's welfare state, the universal family allowance payment, came mainly from the economists in the federal bureaucracy who viewed this policy as a means of maintaining a high level of purchasing power in the economy. In the words of the 1945 White Paper: "The supplementary effect which (family allowances and unemployment insurance) will have on increasing or maintaining employment will ultimately be paid for, in substantial part, out of an increase in income."[24] The subordination of social policy to the goals of economic management within the state also meant the subordination of other social scientists to the economist.

While economics was consolidating its status as the most prestigious of the social sciences, with a special relationship to the state, sociology and political science were developing along very different lines. Sociology was struggling in the 1950s to establish itself as an autonomous field of study within Canadian universities.[25] Unlike in the United States, sociology in English Canada was not called to contribute to the analysis and solution of major social problems. Thus, at the end of the decade the discipline was small, located primarily at McGill University and the University of Toronto; uncertain of its self-image, and particularly of its organizational distinctiveness from economics and anthropology; and only remotely related to the needs of the state. On this last point S. D. Clark has observed: "The concern to dissociate the discipline from any thing having to do with social welfare or social reform had the effect, in my view, of discouraging kinds of research which involved grappling with some of the most serious problems of the society about. When sociologists did undertake studies commissioned by public bodies only too often what was offered in return for the financial support received did little to enhance the reputation of the discipline."[26]

Although political science was considerably more developed than sociology, it experienced somewhat similar difficulties in organizational distinctiveness and in its ability to extend its legitimacy beyond the bounds of academe. The fact that political science typically was grouped with economics in departments of political economy, in which economists dominated both in numbers and in scientific prestige,[27] and that the two Canadian disciplines shared a common professional association and scholarly journal, were manifestations of the political science profession's underdeveloped status. (This is not to imply that the separation of political science from economics has been positive from the standpoint of either discipline's ability to contribute to an understanding of Canadian society. Donald Smiley has observed that one consequence of this separation has been to reinforce the notion that professional economists possess a monopoly over expert advice on matters that concern the economy, a view that the new political economy explicitly rejects and which was quite foreign to the older tradition of political economy in Canada.)[28]

In regard to the relation of the political science community to the state, the discipline had neither the size nor the social prestige of, for example, the scholars associated with France's Fondation nationale de science politique.[29] Part of the reason lay in the colonial condition of the profession in Canada, an impediment to social revelance which only increased as the discipline became, gradually, both institutionalized[30] and influenced by the behaviouralistic political science ascendant in the United Stated during the 1950s and early 1960s. But economics in Canada also was colonized–dominated by personnel trained elsewhere and by models developed for the economies of other countries. And yet the association of Canadian economists with the economics community of "Oxbridge" in the United Kingdom, and with Harvard, Chicago, and other elite schools in the United States, certainly aided the acceptance of their discipline by governments in Canada. The difference in the significance of colonial status for political science as compared to economics can be partially explained by the fact that Western economics, more than any other of the social sciences, had evolved towards an intellectual consensus dominated by the economists of the US and the UK,[31] and had acquired a heavy applied dimension satisfying the requirements of the contemporary capitalist state for technical solutions to policy problems. This is not to minimize debates within economics, but simply to stress that there existed general agreement on a set of fundamental axioms regarding the behavior of agents in the marketplace. Political science on the other hand (and, for that matter, sociology), did not approximate the sort of international consensus that characterized mainstream economics.[32] Model-building and prediction, activities of enhanced value to the state as its planning functions in budgeting and policy making generally reached more sophisticated (though not necessarily more effective) levels, were at the most rudimentary stage in political science and sociology, whereas these had become the main preoccupations of professional economists.

If the relationship between economists and the state in Canada was unparalleled in the case of other social scientists, what of the role of sociologists and political scientists in mobilizing oppositional publics– in other words, in influencing politics through their capacity to shape or articulate the demands of groups opposed to the status quo? The failure of these disciplines to articulate a class critique of Canadian society during the 1950s has already been remarked on. Donald Whyte argues that the relative economic prosperity that was experienced in the decade after World War II did not provide fertile ground for the elaboration of sociological interpretations that stressed class conflict. He goes on to suggest that as the stresses latent in Canada's dependent economic status and in the unequal regional development of the Canadian economy became increasingly evident, the inappropriateness of consensual under-standings of the social system became clear.[32] However, growing nationalism among social scientists in English Canada was not expressed in the forms of *engagement* that characterized their francophone counterparts in Quebec. The reaction that Whyte refers to found expression in the teaching and publications of a growing number of social scientists who accepted the dependency framework developed by Marxist scholars like Andre Gunder Frank.[33] The university itself became an issue in the face of what nationalists argued were the damaging consequences of American influence. But broader political action through parties and organized social movements remained limited. No organ of intellectual dissent as influential as *Cité libre* developed and, with the exception of some limited influence within the national and Saskatchewan CCF-NDP, the link between social scientists and political parties continued to be almost non-existent.

The failure of social science intellectuals to develop connections with the two major national parties requires explanation. Organized as cadre parties in which the membership was mobilized only episodically, and then for support rather than direction, the Liberal and Progressive Conservative parties were dominated in the 1950s by their parliamentary contingents. The extra-parliamentary wings of these parties existed as organizations for raising campaign funds and, in some circumstances, for linking the parliamentary wing of the party to regional constituencies. The irregular convening of elected delegates to select a party leader can hardly be considered a significant channel for extra-parliamentary influence. Nor did the permanent secretariats of the parties provide opportunities for intellectuals to influence party policy. Writing of the secretariat of the Liberal party during the era of Mackenzie King and Louis St. Laurent, Reg Whitaker observes: "It is a mark of the domination of the party leadership as well as the weak level of extra-parliamentary organization in this country that these party bureaucrats never became, as sometimes happened in the European context, 'apparatchicks,' men of indirect but powerful influence on the party."[34]

The structure of opportunities was somewhat more favourable in the CCF, reconstituted as the NDP in 1961. The involvement of the League for Social Reconstruction, an organization modelled after the British Fabian Society and dominated by eastern Canadian intellectuals, in the development of the Regina Manifesto of 1933, the socialist platform of the early CCF, is well known. The participatory principles of the party were reflected in a much greater emphasis on policy sessions and delegate input at gatherings of the CCF, as compared to conventions of the two older parties. However, the influence of intellectuals like Frank Underhill, F.R. Scott, and Eugene Forsey during the early years, when the CCF was as much a social movement as a political party, declined with the CCF's post-war loss of national support. Reduced to a farmers' party, holding power in Saskatchewan, the national CCF moderated its critique of Canadian capitalism and pursued the formal association with organized labour that had always been viewed with ambivalence in the party.[35] The influence of Canadian intellectuals within the country's ideologically moderate labour movement was effectively nil, and the consummation of an organizational link between the CCF and the Canadian Labour Congress through the formation of the NDP in 1961 did nothing to enhance their influence on this social-democratic party. Nevertheless, for left-wing intellectuals there was no other vehicle on the national electoral scene, and many continued to work within the NDP during the 1960s, when American domination of the Canadian economy and cultural penetration became issues of heightened concern among Canadian social scientists.

Saskatchewan under the CCF and NDP governments, in office continuously from 1944 to 1964, provided a test of what might happen when the critics of the social order found themselves in control of the state. As Seymour Martin Lipset observes in *Agrarian Socialism*, the CCF inherited a provincial bureaucracy unused to the policy agenda on which the socialist government was elected.[36] Writing only a few years after the election of the CCF, Lipset argued that the pace of reform had been slowed, and even deliberately stymied, by senior bureaucrats unsympathetic to CCF policies. Moreover, he noted that despite pressure from the party's extra-parliamentary wing for the appointment of "socialist minded persons" to positions in the provincial bureaucracy, the Douglas government moved slowly in replacing high-level civil servants in the existing departmental bureaucracies, though many were in fact patronage appointees of the previous Liberal government. Instead, the Saskatchewan NDP immediately launched into the creation of *new* policy-making structures, attracting to these many ideologically left-wing experts to work for the only avowedly socialist government in North America. At the centre of a new system of technocratic planning was the Economic Advisory and Planning Board, surrounded by the Government Finance Office (the predecessor of the Crown Investments Corporation), the Health Services Planning Commission, and the Budget Bureau.

The effectiveness of the planning that took place under the early CCF governments is a subject on which views differ.[37] What is not in dispute, however, is that the government's commitment to innovation enabled it to attract a coterie of experts who shared the Fabian brand of socialism which characterized the League for Social Reconstruction (LSR).[38] Unlike the technocrats who were recruited into Ottawa to staff the new structures of macro-economic policy, Saskatchewan's new technocracy was not dominated by professional economists. The foremost technocrat under the early Douglas government, George Cadbury, recruited as the first chairman of the Economic Advisory and Planning Board, was a British economist. But other planners included Dr. Mindel Sheps and Dr. Cecil Sheps, Henry Sigerist, Fred Mott, and Len Rosenfeld, all of whom worked in the area of social policy, and T.H. McLeod, who pioneered program budgeting in Saskatchewan through the newly created Budget Bureau. This was almost certainly this country's first inter-disciplinary group of experts operating at the heart of the state. If the credo of the Ottawa mandarins was economic management and their text Keynes's *General Theory*, the credo of the Saskatchewan technocrats was *planning* and their text the LSR's *Social Planning for Canada*. Both groups supported the positive state; but the base of their support, and the forms of state intervention they favoured, were very different.

Social scientists in English Canada constituted during this postwar period what T.S. Eliot termed a clerisy: an establishment of higher learning that through its teaching and research functions reinforced the social order. This was particularly true of economics, which, in addition to its academic activities, established a close relationship to the state as governments assumed increasing responsibility for stabilizing levels of employment and growth in the capitalist economy. The fact that the economics profession was divided between the state and academe both reflected and contributed to the utilitarian orientation of this discipline. Economists were well on their way to becoming the main ideological spokespersons for the existing social order, through their uncritical acceptance of corporate capitalism and their supportive functions as technical experts.

Sociology and political science remained university-based professions, with only a limited and episodic expert relationship to the state. The uncritical acceptance of the main values on which the social order rested and the failure of sociologists and political scientists to contribute to the mobilization of oppositional publics, testified to their functionally conservative role. Regardless of what they subjectively intended, the objective political consequence of their work was not significantly different from that of economists. Disengaged from partisan politics and remote from the centres of decision-making within the state apparatus, sociologists and political scientists existed on the margins of the political process. Not until they developed a critical understanding of Canadian society, linked to the interests of subordinate classes attempting to challenge the structure of economic power in Canada's dependent political economy, would they establish their relevance as agents of political change. This awaited the circumstances of the 1960s.

CHAPTER FIVE

Professional Expansion and Nationalist Dissent, 1963– 1971

With the explosive growth of Canadian universities during the 1960s social science departments were forced to expand in order to meet student enrolments, which doubled between 1960 and 1965. Much of the necessary increase in teaching personnel was supplied from outside the country, particularly from graduate schools in the United States. Along with the sheer increase in the size of the social science community in English Canada there was a proliferation in the number and range of courses offered within each discipline (see table 15). This internal development had two important external consequences: the organizational separation of the economics and political science communities, and the institutionalization of sociology as a distinct field with its own professional associations, journals, and graduate programs.

The respective disciplinary orientations of the social sciences developed along very different lines. The Canadian economics community continued to be, in Harry Johnson's words, a net importer of economic theory,[1] becoming ever more distant from the "political economy" approach associated with Harold Innis and an earlier generation of economists. Indeed, in his retrospective assessment "The State of Economics in Canada,"[2] Johnson has hardly anything to say about *Canadian* contributions to international economic theory, describing instead the course of debates in Anglo-American economics and the institutionalization of the field in Canada. His virulent criticism of dissenters from the classical mainstream of the discipline as ideologically inspired pseudo-intellectuals[3] is only an immoderately heated defense of an orthodoxy that became prevalent in the 1960s. Johnson calls this orthodoxy "scientific economics," as opposed to Marxist and development economics. It involves "the application of logic and quantitative methods to the understanding, interpretation, and prediction of economic phenomena,"[4] and is by its very nature above national traditions. Writing in 1971, Johnson argued that the ability to

Table 15
Profile of Graduate Courses in Economics, Political Science, and Sociology at
the University of Toronto, for Selected Years

Discipline	1950–1	1955–6	1960–1	1965–6	1970–1
Economics					
Theory	2	2	3	4	6.5
History	2	1	2	4	14
Methodology	2	2	2	5	7
Specialized Subjects[a]	12 (4)	7 (2)	9 (3)	14 (7)	21.5 (9.5)
Total	18	12	16	27	49
Political Science					
Theory	2	2	3	2	7
Canadian	1	1	1	5	7.5
Comparative	2	2	4	8	14
International Relations	2	2	2	2	7
Public Administration	–	1	1	1	2
Empirical Methodology	–	–	–	–	1
Total	7	8	11	18	37.5[b]
Sociology					
Theory and General Surveys	2	2	2	5	3
Country and Regional Studies	1	1	1	1	2
Specialized Subjects	1	–	2	10	16
Methodology	1	1	–	1	1
Total	5	4	5	17	22

Source: University of Toronto, *Graduate Studies Calendar*, various years.

[a] The number in parentheses indicates courses with a particular focus on the state, such as public finance, stabilization policy, public utilities economics, economic planning, taxation policy and so forth.
[b] The course entitled "Policy Administration in Developing Countries" has been counted twice; once under comparative and once under public administration. This explains why the column total does not sum to 38.5.

quantify and predict "now constitutes the economists' main claim to superiority as a profession over the general run of intelligent men with an interest in economic problems."[5] With relatively few exceptions, members of Canada's economics community subscribed to the "scientific economics" paradigm defended by Johnson, believing implicitly in the value-neutrality of their professional work.

No such consensus characterized either politial science or sociology during this period of rapid expansion. The importation of behaviouralistic sociology and political science gave rise to a reaction that commingled academic and ideological concerns. Critical understanding of the social and political systems, and the increasing employment of class analysis and dependency theory, contributed to the plurality of approaches within these disciplines. Indeed, it is impossible to speak of the unquestioned dominance of a theoretical model of the sort prevailing in economics. The high expectations which many held for behaviouralism, and for what came to be called "empirical" theory, typically contrasted to "normative" theory, soon were demonstrated to be unrealistic (some would say, misguided; but that raises epistemological questions which are outside the scope of the present study).[6]

From the standpoint of social scientists' relation to the state, the 1960s were significant years in several respects. First, the level of research funding escalated dramatically in the latter half of the decade, increasing more than tenfold between 1965 and 1970. While the total level of funding remained low in comparison to other fields (the Macdonald Committee, inquiring into federal funding of university research, found that in 1967–8 the natural sciences, engineering, and medicine received 84 per cent of all funding, with the remaining 16 per cent going to the social sciences and humanities),[7] the *growth* in funding for the social sciences was more rapid during this period. In the two years from 1965–6 to 1967–8 the total research awards granted by the Canada Council increased fivefold, from $412,000 to $2.1 million. The dramatic annual increases in research funding through the Council, now the Social Sciences and Humanities Research Council, which began in 1965 with the advent of annual appropriations from parliament to supplement the Council's endowment income, peaked in 1970–1. Since then the real value of research support to social scientists outside state organizations has declined by about 25 per cent.[8]

Increased funding by the state raised questions regarding the independence of university researchers. In the social sciences much research continued to be undertaken with only modest research assistance, and often with no external support. Except for contract research (the amounts for which are difficult to determine with any reliability, and which in any case is frequently of limited significance), the Canada Council was and remains the only state agency of any consequence in English Canada funding non-contractual research in the social sciences.[9] In view of the fact that the amounts channelled to the social science community remained relatively small, the danger that research would be unduly influenced by the priorities of a state agency was probably illusory.

A more important development in the relation of political science and sociology to the state was the research conducted by members of these communities for the Royal Commission on Bilingualism and Biculturalism. Although it would be an overstatement to suggest that the B and B Commission did for sociology and political science what the Gordon Commission had done for economics, establishing the legitimacy of a particular field and community of intellectuals in the realm of public policy, nevertheless the level of participation by social scientists (other than economists) in a royal commission of inquiry was unprecedented. Between 1948 and 1963, when the B and B Commission was established, twelve federal royal commissions had dealt with subjects that could reasonably have been considered as falling within the expert competence of social scientists. As table 16 indicates, most of the inquiries that commissioned special studies by social scientists not regularly employed by the state consulted economists. One recalls Frank Underhill's quip that there are two kinds of economists: those who have worked for royal commissions and those who are still hoping to.

The trend toward special studies as a regular part of the inquiry process is clear from this table. This development has been continued by subsequent royal commissions as table 18 in the following chapter demonstrates. It should be added that table 16 understates the participation of economists. Public servants appointed as support staff often were professional economists, and the ranks of commissioners are sprinkled with such notable economists as Harold Innis (Transportation, 1948), O.J. Firestone (Health, 1961), and W.A. Mackintosh (Banking, 1961). One might argue that the pre-eminence of economists was natural enough, given the policy questions addressed by several of these commissions. Such a view attributes to economics a monopoly of competence in regard to the economic life of the country; this attitude is certainly consistent with the increasing specialization and autonomy of the several social sciences. But to define an issue as falling within the exclusive purview of one group of specialists necessarily limits the terms in which the political significance of that issue will be understood. As economics moved toward greater technical sophistication it also became more conservative in its emphasis on the competitive efficiency of markets, at the expense of distributional and other non-efficiency considerations.

It is a fact that (unlike the contributions of sociology and political science) many *non-academics* have done important economic research for royal commissions both as staff members seconded from their regular employers, and as authors of commissioned studies. Table 17 offers a breakdown of published research studies for four royal commissions on economic issues. This provides a rough measure of the relative participation of academics and non-academics.

Table 16
Special Studies for Selected Royal Commissions, 1948–1963

Commission and Years	No. Special Studies	Contribution Disciplines
Transportation, 1948–51	–	–
National Development in the Arts, Letters and Sciences, 1949–51	51	Architecture, Art, Chemistry, Economics, Engineering, History, Journalism, Literature (French and English), Mathematics, Medicine, Music, Philosophy, Psychology, Sociology
Canada's Economic Prospects, 1955–6	33	Economics
Broadcasting, 1955–7	1	Statistical Analysis
Energy, 1957–8	–	–
Transportation, 1959–61	–	–
Automotive Industry, 1960–1	–	–
Government Organization, 1960	–	–
Publications, 1960–1	–	–
Health Services, 1961–5	20	Economics, Sociology
Banking and Finance, 1964	12	Economics
Taxation, 1962–6	26	Economics
Bilingualism and Biculturalism, 1963–9	124	History, Political Science, Psychology, Sociology

Source: Compiled from information in George F. Henderson, *Federal Royal Commissions in Canada, 1867–1966* (Toronto: University of Toronto Press 1967).

Table 17

Academic and Non-Academic Authorship of Published Research for Selected Royal Commissions

	Canada's Economic Prospects 1956	Banking and Finance 1964	Taxation 1966	Corporate Concentration 1978
University-based economists	8	5	17	16[b]
Non-academics from the private sector	17	5	6	13
Non-academics from the public sector	7	2	2	–
Joint works of academics and non-academics	1	–	–	3
Other[a]	–	–	1	1
Total	33	12	26	33

Source: Information contained in the final reports and special studies of these commissions.

[a] The two studies in this category were collective works produced by the research divisions of the commissions.

[b] Six of these studies were on the social implications of corporate concentration, and were carried out by non-economists.

While no pattern of change over time is discernible from the above data, clearly the economic expertise recognized and utilized by the state through royal commissions is not limited to academe.

The B and B Commission marked a significant stage in the relationship of social scientists to the state in two respects. First, the participation of social scientists other than economists in research for the Commission affirmed both their role as experts (as opposed to critics) and the relevance of their disciplines to public policymaking.[10] Second, the B and B Commission continued what John Porter has described[11] as Canada's political obsession with national unity—raising to the status of perhaps the foremost issue on the political agenda the question of how the relationship between Canada's French- and English-language communities affected political integration. In a sense, the social sciences were co-opted into this non-class conception of Canadian politics. It must be acknowledged that a number of studies for the Commission did emphasize the economic dimensions of inequality between the two language groups. But though the evidence of inequality, of mutual misconceptions held by the French and English Canadians toward one another, and of very different socialization experiences contributing to divergent value systems supported the federal government's political resolve to act on the language issue, it certainly did not determine the political outcome. The participation of social scientists in the B and B Commission merely lent a veneer of intellectual legitimacy to the political reforms that were instituted with the passage of the Official Languages Act in 1969. When analyses by social scientists were fundamentally critical of the socio-economic system, or challenged powerful economic interests, as was the case with the *Real Poverty Report*[12] and the Watkins Task Force on Foreign Ownership and the Structure of Canadian Industry, the conditional legitimacy of social-scientific advice in the eyes of Canadian governments was demonstrated very clearly.

By their very nature royal commissions and task forces represented only temporary and *ad hoc* opportunities for social scientists to participate in the political process. During the 1960s the input of social scientists, particularly economists, was institutionalized through the creation of policy advisory organizations both within the state bureaucracy and in the growing para-public sector. This development was part of a larger trend toward the adoption by governments of rational structures of policy-making. The reforms to public sector budgeting inspired by the Report of the Royal Commission on Government Organization and by the example of Planning, Programming, Budgeting (PPB) in the US, as well as and the changes in the system of cabinet decision-making introduced under Pierre Trudeau, were important manifestations of this trend. However, the reforms of particular relevance to social scientists involved the creation of the Economic Council of Canada (ECC) and the Science Council of Canada (SCC): federally funded research bodies with an advisory relationship to the government. In addition, policy analysis units within government departments, typically located at the level of assistant deputy minister, proliferated in response to the new demands imposed by the Treasury Board and the Privy Council Office regarding budgetary submissions.[13]

In retrospect, it appears that neither the ECC nor the SCC represented a significant step in the direction of economic planning. Nor was the influence of social scientists on policy increased in any appreciable way by their association with these bodies. The independence of both the ECC and the SCC from the government of the day, reflected in their organizational separation from the departments and agencies of the state apparatus, was deliberate. At the same time it may have been crippling, in that the research and recommendations generated by these bodies were dissociated from the centres of political power, so that they depended largely on media coverage of their annual reports or special studies for whatever indirect influence they were able to have on policy issues. The ECC, for instance, was neither intended as, nor did it evolve into, the counterpart of the President's Council of Economic Advisors in the US. There was, of course, some overlapping of membership between the bureaucratic, political, and intellectual elites; but this was an informal network, not strong enough to overcome the structural weaknesses that beset the advisory agencies.

Since its formation in 1963 the ECC has been headed by a chairperson and two directors, who have been trained economists, and the orientation of the Council's professional staff always has been solidly in the mainstream of the Canadian economics community. Much of the ECC's early work was in the development of tools of economic analysis and prediction: notably, the CANSIM computerized data bank for economic time-series analysis, the macro-economic model of the Canadian economy known as CANDIDE; social indicators; and policy evaluation techniques,[14] thereby reinforcing the expert role of the economics profession in the state. More recently the ECC has been one of the organizations most vocal in support of freer trade with the United States, increased competition in heavily regulated sectors of the Canadian economy, and the privatization of crown corporations, a strategy for economic recovery which varies sharply from the economic planning approach advocated by the SCC.

In the case of the Science Council of Canada, its preoccupation with applied science and technology led it quite naturally to support state promotion of research and development and, more generally, an industrial strategy in support of high-technology sectors of the economy. From its inception in 1966 the SCC has been a consistent advocate of centralized industrial planning, and has advanced a nationalist critique of dependence upon external sources of research and development. The participation of social scientists (mainly economists) in special studies for the council has been almost exclusively on the issue of an industrial strategy, and did not begin until the early 1970s. Indeed, the original identification of the Council's mandate with the natural and applied sciences inevitably was broadened to include matters of concern to social scientists as the inter-relatedness of problems in a complex society quickly became evident to researchers associated with the SCC. Bruce Doern writes: "In part, the term "science policy" is a misnomer, a fact the council quickly discovered when it decided that it had to look at broad social policies and goals. The 1969–70 annual report reveals this even more clearly. Scarcely a single social issue escapes mention ... Perhaps it was inevitable that a council given a scanning role would wander into the totality of social problems ..."[15] Thus, the SCC came to be an institutional channel for the articulation of an approach to social problems requiring state intervention and some degree of central planning. However, the peripheral political significance of the science and technology community and (as in the case of the ECC) the fact that the council was dissociated from the structures of policy making were principal factors that prevented the SCC from becoming an influential critic of social and economic policies. Compared to advisory councils such as France's Conseil économique et social, Belgium's Conseil économique central, and the Netherlands' Social and Economic Council, all of which are linked in systematic ways to the executive in the policymaking process, the ECC and SCC hardly can be said to have been integral parts of an economic planning system.

Neither the ECC nor the SCC provided expanded opportunities for sociologists and political scientists to participate as experts in the policy process. Both agencies have from time to time sponsored studies by social scientists who were not economists, but this has been infrequent. Sociology and political science remained overwhelmingly academic in their professional orientation, while the institutional reforms of the 1960s further consolidated (though mainly in symbolic terms) the special relationship of economics to public policy. The creation in the 1970s of several non-governmental institutes for policy research, as well as changes in the cabinet committee system, would inject a measure of pluralism into the organizational network of policy advice, bringing "unorthodox" economists and other social scientists into the process. However, as will be argued in the following chapter, the pre-eminence of mainstream economics in the policy-making process has persisted.

The developments in the social sciences, the university system, and the structures of policy-making described in the preceding pages occurred during a period in which the stresses engendered by Canada's dependent political economy led to increased nationalism among social scientists.[16] The high levels of foreign ownership in the domestic economy and the significance of this for industrial development and political sovereignty were the main issues in this nationalist critique. The cultural dimension of Canada's dependent relationship to the United States found a rallying point in the writings of the philosopher George Grant.[17] His argument that Canada had fallen irretrievably into the orbit of the homogenizing technology of American capitalism, while expressed in terms of a conservative nostalgia, produced a sympathetic resonance among left-leaning intellectuals. Another strand of this nationalism decried the influence of American values within Canadian universities. It was argued that the high proportion of non-Canadians, particularly Americans, hired during the rapid expansion of the university system and the dependence of social science departments in English Canada on the products of American graduate schools represented an insidious form of cultural imperialism.[18] While this issue was largely contained within the university community, generating an acrimonious and frequently personal debate, its broader political significance rested in the opposing conceptualizations of the class position of social science intellectuals.

To understand this, it must be recalled that the period of the late 1960s witnessed a breakdown in the economic dimension of the so-called "special relationship" between the governments of Canada and the US. This was due mainly to measures taken by US administrations in reaction to American balance of payments problems and the exigencies of financing an escalated war effort in Vietnam. The American practice of extraterritoriality, in extending of the requirements of the American state to Canadian subsidiaries of US-based corporations (and therefore placing limitations on the economic and political choices available to Canadian decision-makers), increasingly became a cause for concern and reinforced the argument to expand control over its domestic economic activity. Moreover, evidence that the structure of Canadian industry was a miniature replica of the American industrial economy, and that levels of research and development in, and exports by, Canada's manufacturing sector were low focused attention on the causes of this apparent industrial underdevelopment and on the relationship between the political and economic systems. The nationalist understanding attributed this under-development to the behavior of foreign capital in Canada. Mainstream economists acknowledged many of the same symptoms, but attributed them to long-standing Canadian government restrictions on competition (principally through tariff policy).[19]

The controversy over the economic and political effects of foreign ownership has been examined on a number of occasions.[20] The writings of economic nationalists such as Kari Levitt, Charles Taylor, Abraham Rotstein, Robert Laxer, Mel Watkins, and others, focused on the monopoly power of the large US-based multinational corporations operating in Canada.[21] At the political level this critique was articulated by the NDP and by the Committee for an Independent Canada. Nationalist social scientists were active in both of these organizations. The economic na-tionalist critique had sufficient support to compel the appointment of three government inquiries into the consequences of foreign ownership: the Task Force on Foreign Ownership and the Structure of Canadian Industry (the Watkins Report, 1968); the Task Force on Foreign Direct Investment in Canada (the Gray Report, 1972); and the Ontario Select Commission on Cultural and Economic Nationalism (1973).[22]

The dependency framework argued by nationalists did not become the dominant model in the social sciences for understanding the Canadian economy and society. With the exception of enclaves of political economists at the universities of Toronto and Manitoba, it made virtually no headway in the economics community. Increasing numbers of sociologists and political scientists adopted its critical perspective; but even the most casual perusal of learned journals and papers delivered at annual meetings of the CPSA and the Canadian Sociology and Anthropology Association (CSAA) shows that acceptance of the nationalist framework was far from unanimous. Nevertheless, signs of political economy's revitalization, at least in sociology and political science, existed, and injected into the social sciences a critical element that had been relatively rare in the previous decade.[23] The nationalism issue provided the basis for both critique and *engagement* on the part of many social scientists.

The nationalism debate raised fundamentally important questions about the class position of intellectuals. The critique of foreign ownership and of the dependent structure of the Canadian economy implied specific remedies, including an expansion of state intervention to challenge the dominance of foreign capital. On this statist implication Donald Whyte has written: "Whether wittingly or not, many social scientists who took up the national challenge during the 1960s and 1970s gave ideological support to the growth in scope and power of the state system. What the nationalist debate reflected in Canada was the confrontation, in ideological form, of the various fragments of the bourgeoisie, organized around the federal and provincial states and vying with each other for pre-eminence in defining universal priorities."[24] Whyte's interpretation overstates the federalism dimension, which was important principally in the case of French Canadian intellectuals. It is fair enough to argue that the bourgeoisie in Canada was fragmented on regional lines, but the rifts among social scientists on this issue are more properly understood in terms of their conceptualization of Canadian society and the role of the state *in general*, irrespective of the level of government.

Within the universities the nationalism issue tended to assume the form of a debate over American influences on the social sciences in English Canada. The economic nationalism critique was often linked to calls for an autonomous Canadian social science, purged of what were argued to be the ideological baggage of the positivistic behaviouralism and general ethnocentrism of the social sciences in the United States. Left-wing social scientists, who criticized the considerable presence of non-Canadians in the universities and the general importation of "American" theories and approaches, often conceived of their social role as bound up with the liberation of subordinate classes in Canada.[25] Of these tendencies Alan Cairns has observed, in the particular case of political science: "Most of the existing arguments for a degree of distinctiveness in Canadian political science either are political in their attempts to cast political scientists in a particular partisan role in the Canadian polity, or they simply express preferences for one disciplinary tendency over another and attempt to use national labels and boundaries to shore up the preferred position."[26] Indeed, calls for a nationalistic social science ran directly counter to the widely held view that scientific inquiry, by definition, ought to be non-national.[27] In any case, the particular controversy over Americanization of the universities had little impact outside of academe, and the maturation in Canada of graduate programs in the social sciences during the 1970s reduced its immediacy.

Nationalism and the Watkins Report provided the rallying point for the intellectual left that state planning and the Rowell-Sirois Report[28] had for the critical intellectuals associated with the LSR and the *Canadian Forum* three decades earlier. The parallel obviously is not exact. One of the main differences between the two cases was in their intellectual inspiration: the LSR took root in a combination of Fabian socialism, the Christian "social gospel" movement, and progressivism (the belief in the possibility and desirability of improving the human condition, and using the state to achieve these ends); the nationalist left of the 1960s borrowed extensively from Marxist scholarship, and dependency theory and was in large part a reaction against American economic and cultural influences. But both groups of intellectuals constitute the main source of criticism of the social order in their respective periods. In neither case, however, did the critical interpretation of Canadian society achieve dominance in academic circles. And in each case the political influence of left-wing intellectuals was marginal. Yet despite their exclusion from the intellectual and political mainstream, they certainly were the aspiring vanguard, if any existed in Canada of the 1930s or the 1960s. Any attempt to discover perspectives in the social sciences that fundamentally challenged the dominant social order must inevitably focus on Canada's intellectual left.

The generally uncritical and disengaged orientation that had characterized the social science community during the previous two decades was challenged increasingly during the 1960s by interpretations of Canadian society that stressed conflict. These challenges arose principally within the burgeoning fields of political science and sociology. Economics continued to evolve towards a unified theory of choice in individual rather than class terms, and therefore accepted the basic property values and liberal ideology on which capitalist relations of production are based. However, the critical perspectives generated by social scientists working within dependency, nationalistic, and class frameworks were largely unsuccessful in mobilizing public opposition in the broader political system— perhaps for want of organizations able or willing to transform critique into action. The NDP embraced the economic nationalist critique; but, as events leading up to the expulsion of the radical "Waffle" wing of the party would demonstrate, the majority sentiment in the NDP was that the party's popularity should not be threatened by policy positions that lacked the support of such constituencies as organized labour. With the exception of the wing of Canadian capital represented by Walter Gordon in the Liberal Party,[29] the two older parties were stony ground for economic nationalism.

Institutional developments in the Canadian state apparatus reinforced the expert relationship of economists to the state. Economics in Canada continued to develop along the same lines as in the United States, namely, toward greater technical sophistication and less diversity in methodology and theoretical premises. These trends were reflected in the applied work going on in the discipline: modelling, forecasting, and the development of economic indicators and methods of policy evaluation. This technology was of clear utility to the interventionist state. On the other hand, political scientists and sociologists, despite their extensive participation in special studies for the B and B Commission, remained overwhelmingly academic in orientation and remote from centres of policymaking. But at the same time, sociology and political science were evolving towards greater pluralism in approaches. A fair barometer of this difference is evident in introductory textbooks used in the respective fields. Whereas teaching in economics was dominated by Paul Samuelson's *Economics* (which had reached its eighth edition by 1970)[30] and Lipsey and Steiner's *Economics*,[31] no such comprehensive text, expressing a coherent and generally accepted analytical framework, existed in either political science or sociology. One could reasonably speak of a dominant theoretical paradigm in economics; but this was impossible in the other social sciences.

Without undue simplification it can be said that economists working out of a dependency framework and political economists, all of which were fringe groups within the profession) economists had become a clerisy linked to the dominant segment of the capitalist class. This segment was not nationalist, but rather represented trans-national capital, and therefore stood for the elimination of trade and competition policies that viewed the economy within national boundaries.[32] The class position of sociologists and political scientists was more complex. The emergence of critical currents within these disciplines, particularly the economic nationalism critique, challenged the conventional view of Canada as a society in which class divisions were unimportant. Beginning in a major way with the publication of John Porter's *The Vertical Mosaic* the traditional preoccupation with the accommodation of diverse regional, linguistic and other group interests was increasingly argued to be divisive. Creative politics, in which political alignments and discourse would be in terms of social class, was advocated as both a remedy for these divisive tendencies, and as a step toward increasing the political influence of subordinate classes.[33] While the clerisy of the economists moved further away from a concern for the distributional consequences of economic structures, that very concern was central to the critical understanding advanced by sociologists and political scientists working out of a political economy framework. However, the influence of the political economy approach within sociology and political science during the 1960s should not be exaggerated. With an electoral system that discouraged class alignments, and in the absence of politically significant supportive constituencies–a working class capable of being mobilized, or an ascendant middle class as in Quebec–the political impact of these left-wing social scientists was insubstantial in English Canada.

CHAPTER SIX

A Stymied Vanguard and Consolidation of the Expert Role, 1971–1986

The social sciences continued to grow during the early 1970s; but a downturn in undergraduate enrolments and financial cutbacks by the federal and provincial governments resulted in a levelling off by the middle of the decade. The nationalist critique of Canada's dependent relationship with the US, and of the "Americanization" of Canadian universities as a microcosm of this colonized status, claimed an increasing number of followers among sociologists and political scientists, and found public expression in such journals of contemporary opinion as *Canadian Forum*, *Canadian Dimension*, *Our Generation*, and *This Magazine*. The Report of the Task Force on Foreign Direct Investment, issued in 1972, was generally supportive of the economic dependency analysis, though its recommendations were less extensive than those proposed by the nationalist left. Kari Levitt, one of the major figures on the intellectual left, was optimistic about political developments: "There is today [1972] a wave of economic nationalism moving through English Canada. Initiated by Walter Gordon, continued by Melville Watkins–from the Watkins Report to the Waffle movement–it is gathering increasing support from all sections of the population. There is a feeling that it is time to put a finish to our traditional attitudes of impotence and inferiority vis-à-vis all things American. There are strong currents of opinion within both the Conservative and the Liberal parties and one has the impression that they are jostling for moderate and safe planks on a nationalist election bandwagon."[1]

But despite these indications of continued vitality, left-wing nationalism experienced a major setback with the defeat of the Waffle movement at the NDP national leadership convention in 1971, and its subsequent expulsion from the party. The Waffle is perhaps best characterized as the non-establishment wing of a political party that was used to viewing itself as ranged against the established powers in Canadian society. Those identified with the movement claimed that the more moderate, "establishment" members of the NDP were inclined to sacrifice ideology and hard positions on issues for political expediency. (The name was a deliberate attempt at irony, as those who were part of the movement were critical of others in the NDP who, they claimed, "waffled" on the issues.) The majority's decision to reject what they considered extreme policy positions that prejudiced the party's electoral competitiveness deprived nationalist intellectuals of an organizational vehicle for mobilizing popular opinion.

The Waffle and its leadership candidate, James Laxer, advocated the nationalization of all resource industries and the extension of public ownership in other sectors of the economy. As Michael Cross noted in a post-convention assessment, the Waffle proposed state capitalism as the solution to foreign control of the domestic economy. This proposal was based on the view that the economic imperialism of foreign (mainly American), capital was the root cause of such problems as the non-competitiveness of Canada's manufacturing sector in international markets, and the heavy reliance on natural resource industries.[2] The Waffle's anti-imperialism also was expressed in its support for the right of French Canadians in Quebec to self-determination. Proposed policy resolutions on both of these issues were rejected by the convention in favour of more moderate positions. However, the very fact that these issues were debated had important consequences, polarizing the leadership competition on ideological lines, and exposing the long-standing tension between ideology and "pragmatism" in the NDP. After four ballots, David Lewis emerged with a narrow victory over James Laxer.

It would be an oversimplistic distortion to argue that this tension, and the eventual choice between David Lewis and James Laxer on the final leadership ballot, pitted the "workers" against the "eggheads" in the party, particularly in view of the fact that such important NDP intellectuals as Charles Taylor and Desmond Morton were Lewis supporters. Nevertheless, the convention confirmed a drift that had been evident in the party since the diluted socialism of the Winnipeg Declaration (1956) had replaced the Regina Manifesto (1933) as the CCF's statement of principles; this tendency was reinforced through the formal association of the NDP with ideologically conservative organized labour in 1961. With the party's decision to expel the Waffle faction, the NDP establishment demonstrated its support for Desmond Morton's assessment of the convention's significance: "Our business as New Democrats ... is to win power for our ideas."[3] It was felt that this could not be done on the nationalist platform advocated by the Waffle, and indeed that the NDP could not afford to face the electorate without having repudiated ideological radicalism. Precisely when Kari Levitt was professing to see signs of increasing popular support for the economic nationalists' ideas, the most likely instrument for their dissemination on the hustings and in parliament was effectively distancing itself from the ideological position associated with the nationalist critique.

Unlike their counterparts in Quebec, left-wing intellectuals in English Canada were unable to articulate an analysis of Canadian society that expressed the interests of an ascendant class. Social scientists in Quebec, particularly sociologists, succeeded in defining Quebec as a distinct national society, a conceptualization that supported province-building activities which expanded the career opportunities of a growing francophone middle class, and that was successful precisely for this reason. Circumstances in English Canada were substantially different. Language did not place anglophones at a competitive disadvantage for jobs and upward socio-economic mobility. The mobilization of subordinate groups in support of a dependency analysis of Canadian society was impeded by the disorganizing effect of non-class cleavages and a dominant liberal ideology that stressed individual mobility rather than structured inequality.[4] Quebec of the 1960s was a society in the throes of a profound transformation of its social structure, changes that had been developing during the industrialization of the previous decades.[5] With the eclipse of the ideological hegemony of the Catholic church, social scientists became important participants in defining a modernized society. Because English Canada was undergoing no such social upheaval, the traditional liberal conceptualization of Canadian society was not nearly as vulnerable to the challenges of the left.

The nationalist critique of Canada as a dependent society locked into a subordinate relationship to the United States was not abandoned by left wing social scientists, despite the lack of sympathetic response by the political parties and organized labour. Instead, the critique experienced a sort of involution, developing within the universities and in leftist periodicals such as *This Magazine* as a new version of political economy. While linking itself to the tradition of such figures as Innis, Fowke, and Mackintosh, the new political economy made extensive use of Marxist concepts, welding to metropolitanism the dependency theory developed by André Gunder Frank in his study of Latin America. Within the Canadian Political Science Association a Political Economy section was established, and the formation of the journal *Studies in Political Economy* (1978) provided a scholarly outlet for the work of left-wing social scientists. It is tempting to see in the proliferation of theoretical and empirical work in Marxist-dominated political economy since the early 1970s a reaction to nationalist social scientists' failure to make inroads in the political system. Nevertheless, what is important in the context of the present study is that the new political economy has had little impact beyond intellectual circles. Its logically supportive constituencies—marginal socioeconomic groups and peripheral regions—are not easily mobilized, and the critical ideology of the social scientists working within this framework precludes an expert relationship to the state.

On this last point, the trend toward the integration of social scientists into the policy-making process, described in the previous chapter, has continued. Richard French has described in considerable detail the decision-making reforms instituted by Liberal governments during the 1970s.[6] He identifies three distinct planning systems, each linked to a different central agency and each having a particular disciplinary orientation: (1) the Finance Planning System (classical macroeconomics); (2) the Treasury Planning System (applied microeconomics, management science); and (3) the Cabinet Planning system (policy sciences). French argues that a series of economic and political crises, from the imposition of wage and price controls in October 1975 to the end of the decade, compelled reactive policymaking, undermining the possibility of rational policy-making. This did not mean that the intellectual bases of the three planning systems were discredited. Rather, it demonstrated both the practical obstacles to such a process and the absence of a single intellectual framework within which a consensus on the desirability of planning, with its statist implications, could be reached.

While it has become popular to speak of the fall of rational policy-making with the apparent failure of the reforms undertaken during the Trudeau era, this should not be taken to signify a decline in the uses (symbolic and substantive) made of social-scientific information by the state. In a recent article on "Sociology and the Nationalist Challenge in Canada," Donald Whyte refers to an internal study of senior management in several departments of the federal government which reveals that "the most frequently utilized discipline for knowledge about the external environment was sociology."[7] He argues that "the extension of state initiatives into qualitative aspects of society and the importance of human capital to economic growth have brought sociologists and anthropologists into research and consultative capacities previously reserved for economists."[8] Certainly it is the case that such departments as Health and Welfare, Indian Affairs and Northern Development, and the Solicitor General's office have made extensive use of the work of sociologists, anthropologists, and social psychologists, both as staff members and as consultants. There can be little doubt, however, that economists remain pre-eminent among social scientists in their integration with the policy process. Indeed, it is difficult to conceive of a volume of essays similar to the C.D. Howe Institute's *Economic Policy Advising in Canada*[9] in the case of either sociology or political science.

During this recent period in the postwar evolution of the relationship between social scientists and politics a number of policy research institutes have been created. These include the Vancouver-based Fraser Institute (supported mainly through business contributions); the C.D. Howe Institute (established in 1973 from the merger of the C.D. Howe Memorial Foundation and the Private Planning Association of Canada); the Institute for Research on Public Policy (the IRPP is an independent organization established in 1972 and supported by the federal and provincial governments and private sector contributors); the Canadian Institute for Economic Policy (disbanded in 1984); and the Canadian Council on Social Development (whose focus is social policy). The Conference Board, a New York-based research institute supported by corporate contributors, has continued to operate in Canada, producing (among other things) quarterly analyses of the Canadian economy and its prospects. The orientations of these organizations vary according to their areas of concern, the sorts of social scientists they typically employ, and their ideological character. The Fraser Institute describes its objective as "the redirection of public attention to the role of competitive markets in providing for the well-being of Canadians."[10] Its free-enterprise philosophy is generally expressed in publications written by economists, while ideologically the Institute is heir to the liberalism of F.A. Hayek, who in fact was one of the original members of the institute's editorial board. Both the C.D. Howe Institute and the Conference Board are concerned with economic policy issues, providing non-governmental channels for policy advice, primarily from economists. The now-defunct Canadian institute for Economic Policy, while dealing with many of the same issues as the other economic policy institutes, tended to be more sympathetic to industrial planning. Its publications included several by non-economists (or, in some cases, unorthodox economists), including Richard French's *How Ottawa Decides*, Stephen Clarkson's *Canada and the Reagan Challenge*, Hugh Thorburn's *Planning and the Economy*, and Abraham Rotstein's *Rebuilding from Within*. IRPP has the broadest range of policy concerns of these non-governmental policy institutes, consistent with its mandate to "act as a catalyst within the national community by helping to facilitate informed public debate on issues of major public interest."[11] Its published research includes the work of economists, political scientists, and sociologists, and indeed the IRPP represents one of a dwindling number of channels in Canada for the publication of monographs on contemporary public policy.

Two points need to be made regarding these policy research institutes. First, most of them take the economy, and whatever affects its performance, as their principal object of study, publishing mainly the analyses of professional economists. Their activities have thus reinforced the belief that these matters fall only within the expert purview of professional economists, thereby reinforcing the special relationship of economics to the policy process. Second, the influence of these organizations, like that

Table 18
Special Studies for Selected Royal Commissions, 1967–1985

Commission and Years	No. Special Studies	Contributing Disciplines
Status of Women, 1967–70	34	Anthropology, Economics, History, Law, Psychology, Sociology
Corporate Concentration, 1975–8	33	Economics, Industrial Relations, Law, Political Science, Sociology
Newspapers, 1980–1	32	Economics, Journalism, Law, Political Science
Economic Union and Development Prospects for Canada, 1982–85	72	Economics, Law, Political Science
Equality in Employment, 1985	29	Economics, Law, Sociology

of the ECC and the SCC, is largely dependent upon media coverage of their analyses and recommendations. In some cases there may be an informal relationship between an institute and political decision-makers. Such a direct line of influence has been argued to exist between the Fraser Institute and British Columbia's current Social Credit government.[12]

Royal Commissions would appear to have provided greater opportunities for non-economists to participate as policy experts. Since the B and B Commission there have been five major federal royal commissions that could reasonably have been expected to draw on a range of social scientific research support. These commissions, and the disciplines contributing to the research studies done for them, are indicated in table 18.

Research support by social scientists has become a standard part of the royal commission process. The near-hegemony of economics that characterized royal commission research before the B and B Commission has been broken—though close inspection of the studies undertaken for these later royal commissions reveals that economists, by the proportion of research they account for, continue to dominate. Task forces provide another channel for the participation of social scientists—though they have preferred hearing expert testimony *in camera* to commissioning research studies for publication. The Task Force on Canadian Unity (1977–9) is perhaps the major instance of social scientists' involvement. It had as its three chief advisors professors Léon Dion, John Meisel, and Edward

McWhinney, all prominent political scientists. In addition to its public hearings, the task force held numerous private meetings with economists, political scientists, sociologists, and professors of law and of English. It produced a document, *Coming to Terms: The Words of the Debate*, that drew heavily upon the contributions of these experts.[13]

The important question, in the context of the present study, is whether the participation of social scientists in royal commissions and task forces involves legitimation. Is their research merely applied, in order to lend the weight of "disinterested" analysis to a policy choice that either was already decided upon or was determined by very different factors? Or does their participation contribute to the conceptualization of the policy problem and therefore to the action ultimately taken? Conceptualization means that social science research may sensitize policy makers to relationships and consequences of which they were not aware, and that the findings of such research may also become common knowledge, influencing "the way that a society thinks about issues, the facets of the issues that are viewed as susceptible to alteration, and the alternative measures that it considers."[14] In fact, legitimation and conceptualization are not mutually exclusive consequences. However, the real influence that social scientists can bring to bear on policy by participating in such bodies probably is demonstrated in the case of the Royal Commission on Taxation (1962–6). Grounded largely on the work of university-based economists, the Commission's report recommended significant reform of the structure of taxation in Canada. It is generally conceded that these recommendations, which were embodied in modified form in the federal government's White Paper on Taxation (1970), had little, if any, impact on public policy. The issue of tax reform was resolved through the interaction of vested interests and governments.[15] Similarly, the fact that many of the research studies carried out for the recent Macdonald Commission are supportive of some sort of free-trade arrangement with the US would appear to be incidental to the federal government's decision to pursue talks with the US administration toward this end. Dissenting research such as the industrial strategy option recommended by economist Richard Harris in a study prepared for the Commission,[16] is unlikely to have any effect on policy, except to act as a focus for such sympathetic interests as high technology industry and organized labour.

The participation of social scientists in the Task Force on National Unity, mentioned above, raises the question of their role in the debate over Quebec's status within Canadian federalism. With the election of the Parti Québécois government on 15 November 1976, a government committed to holding a referendum on what amounted to associate statehood for Quebec, the issue of Quebec separatism gained immediacy. The period leading up to the May 1980 referendum on sovereigntyassociaton was marked by a spate of conferences with such titles as *Options Canada* and *Alternatives Canada* (both held at the University of Toronto in October 1977), in which academics participated extensively. Within months of the election of the PQ a group of academics, mainly political scientists at Queen's University, produced a volume of essays entitled *Must Canada Fail?* In explaining the book's purpose and its *engagé* tenor, the editor wrote: "As teachers, we have in preparing this book felt uneasy at our departure from analytic detachment, and our willingness to rush into print before all the research is in. But time moves fast, and we, like all citizens, must make our voices heard before it is too late to do anything but write history."[17]

While the response of English Canadian social scientists was certainly not unanimous, there was considerable sympathy for the position that greater autonomy for Quebec, perhaps the *statut particulier* advocated by Claude Ryan,[18] was a just and necessary response to the demands presented by the PQ. Support for *indépendantisme*, or at least the more moderate option of special status for Quebec within Canada, was not restricted to left wing intellectuals who viewed Quebec as a dependent society. In *Canada in Question: Federalism in the Eighties*, Donald Smiley wrote: "It may be that when Canadians in both Quebec and outside that province come to look at the alternatives cool-headedly they will decide that the creation of two or more jurisdictions possessing sovereignty in the fullest legal sense would be less than calamitous."[19] David Kwavnick has argued that many political scientists and sociologists in English Canada effectively caused confusion in the debate by accepting the premises of the Quebec nationalists: the identity of French Canada with Quebec, the idea of Quebec as a national society, and the questionable logic of national self-determination.[20] The federal government's reaction to such arguments was its repudiation of the decentralist analysis contained in the Report of the Task Force on National Unity, and its rejection of the Quebec Liberal Party's Beige Paper recommending special status for Quebec.

With the passage of the Canada Act (1982) and the weakening of the *indépendantiste* movement in Quebec, the national unity issue receded into the background. Concern among social scientists with French-English relations and the structure of federalism was overshadowed by economic issues: chronic high unemployment, a deteriorating balance of trade, a burgeoning federal deficit, and reduced levels of new investment in the economy.[21] Indeed, dozens of the most prominent economists and political scientists in Canada were engaged by the recent Macdonald Commission on the economy. Frank Underhill's characterization of academics who work for royal commissions as the garage mechanics of capitalism is perhaps unfair to some of the social scientists who worked for this particular commission, although Daniel Drache and Duncan Cameron, the editors of *The Other Macdonald Report*, argue that "the academic consultants chosen by the commission held views that largely coincided with those of the business agenda. This reflects the fact that the social science disciplines naturally take their agenda from the dominant concerns of society–and in a liberal democratic society, business concerns are dominant."[22]

But is it a "fact" that the agenda of the social sciences "naturally" is determined by the interests of the "dominant concerns in society"? The evidence does not lend unequivocal support to such an interpretation. The overwhelming (but not unanimous) support for the removal of restrictions on trade and the unregulated working of markets expressed by the economists working for the Macdonald Commission must be viewed alongside the critical perspectives advanced by those social scientists who were *not* asked to do research for the commission–as well as those whose conclusions did not find their way into the final report. Richard Simeon, a Queen's political scientist who was a research coordinator with the Macdonald Commission, argues that the decision to organize the commission's research work into three main divisions according to discipline (economics, political science, and law) had serious consequences for the research work carried out in support of the commissioners' decision-making. It meant not only that certain perspectives were excluded but also that the likelihood of interdisciplinary perspectives on economic problems was remote, given that each discipline effectively had a research monopoly in a particular area. The commissioners understood their task to be the development of solutions to the problems of Canada's slow economic growth, its declining international competitiveness, and its vulnerability to economic and political developments in the US because of its trade dependence. The segmented organization of the Commission's research, along with the relative unanimity of views expressed by economists and their willingness to make confident recommendations for change, combined to reinforce among the commissioners a belief that the economists were the only social scientists with a legitimate claim to scientific expertise on how to improve Canada's economic situation.[23]

Over the last several years links have developed between many social scientists (particularly those working out of the political economy framework that emphasizes the political significance of economic power and its unequal distribution) and various social organizations that view the economy from the standpoint of peripheral groups in Canadian society. The critique of capitalism and conventional economic policy issued by Canada's Catholic bishops in their 1983 New Year's statement, "Ethical Reflections on the Economic Crisis," generally received a positive reception from left-wing social scientists, at the same time as it was dismissed by mainstream economists and many politicians as inexpert nonsense.[24] Its relevance to the present study lies in the fact that the "option for the poor," advocated by the Canadian bishops and viewed sympathetically by some other church organizations in Canada,[25] involved criticisms of public policy and the distribution of power in society which were fundamentally similar to those made by the new political economy. This common ground between left-wing intellectuals and the ethical concerns of the churches recalls the original basis of the CCF. Drache and Cameron write: "In a period when Canadian society is supposedly shifting to the right, there are more forces ready for social change than either the general public or the traditional left can recognize. The proof of its existence is the coalitions that have been built in the Solidarity effort in British Columbia, the court challenge to cruise missile testing, the defence of abortion rights, the Eaton's boycott and the Social Policy Reform Group. The groups active in these coalitions are Canada's counter-institutions, and they draw on a counter-discourse of political economy."[26]

However, this "counter-discourse" has not yet led to the *politically effective* mobilization of the peripheral groups whose interests it argues are excluded by the current structure of power, and ignored by social scientists who in acting as policy experts rather than social critics lend support to this structure. Despite Drache and Cameron's sweeping assertion that a popular consensus exists on economic policy, and that it is based on the same social justice concerns that have been articulated by the churches, the nature of this consensus appears to take the form of dissent from the policies of recent governments, rather than agreement on an alternative social vision.

Social Scientists and Politics: Conclusion on the Differences between French and English Canada

In examining the political significance of social scientists in Quebec and English Canada in the period covered by this study, we have considered the forms and the extent of their political involvement, their relations with the state, and their class position as intellectuals. Not unexpectedly, these dimensions of political involvement were found to differ significantly between the two communities of social science intellectuals, a fact explained largely by the pre-eminence of the national question in French Canada and the particular circumstances of socio-economic modernization and political transformation which came together during the Quiet Revolution. Indeed, comparison of Quebec and English Canada provides insights into the factors that shape the relation of social scientists to politics, disclosing a complex interplay of forces which precludes any neat, deterministic formulation of this relation. Before attempting to draw some of the broader conclusions that emerge from this study, a summary of developments in the political significance of the social sciences in Canada is necessary.

The first period (1943–59) identified in this study may be characterized as *the struggle for legitimacy* of the social sciences in Quebec: a period marked by their professional institutionalization and their growing social prestige. This process resulted from the interaction of many factors. First, the regime in power and the conservative ideologists that supported it could neither mask their increasing incapacity to cope with the times nor stop the erosion of their social dominance. While intellectuals in the social sciences were the vanguard of this process, demolishing the obfuscations of the conservative ideology and preparing an alternative to it, opposition to the *vieux régime* cut across Quebec society as a whole. It is because of their broad social basis that the anti-Duplessis forces deserve to be characterized as a social movement. Intellectuals had an undeniable self-interest in restructuring social relationships and political power in

Quebec society. Some other social groups and classes, however, shared this interest; and indeed, their political involvement was not free from self-interested concerns. The success of Quebec's francophone social scientists in consolidating their professional status in the universities and challenging the ideology and power structure of pre-Quiet Revolution Quebec owed much to the coincidence of their interests with those of the socially ascendant new middle class.

The new intellectuals at Laval University acquired their professional training and their ideology of social reform outside Quebec. Through the process of disqualifying non-specialized teaching staff, the secularization of the social sciences proceeded during this period from Catholic social philosophy to positivist methods of inquiry. The new generation of professionally-trained social scientists translated into Québécois terms the predominant North American model of social development, using it as both a theoretical framework and as a counter-ideology. It was this double nature of the positivist social science developed at Laval that made academic activity a subversive act and social involvement practically unavoidable. By the same token, as the social sciences became institutionalized it became necessary to separate academic activity from social involvement to avoid endangering the independence of the social sciences by too closely identifying them with particular social groups or organizations. Finally, the achievement of mature professional status also meant the establishment of a system of self-regulated production and reproduction of intellectual goods and agents.

The second period (1960–9) may be characterized as *legitimacy on the march*. In the Quiet Revolution the goals advocated by social scientists were implemented: the expansion of the role of the state; reforms in education and in the social services; the establishment of several state enterprises; and the adoption of technocratic planning and *animation sociale* under the banner of the ideology of *rattrapage*. All these reforms met real social needs. They also opened a new array of positions for members of Quebec's new middle class, thus demonstrating the affinity of its interests to those of the expanding community of social scientists. As in English Canada, the university system expanded tremendously. This expansion had implications beyond academe. It increased the university's social importance, and indeed the need for trained cadres to fill positions in the growing public sector was one of the driving forces behind this growth. Social scientists found two complementary avenues open to them. They could move into positions in the expanding university system or they could assume positions in the growing provincial state and in the field of social planning.

The ideology of the new middle class to which the social science intellectuals were allied contained, however, the seeds of contradiction.

Discrepancies between the idealistic discourse of the social sciences and the imperfect reality of the reforms instituted during the Quiet Revolution led to divisions among those who only a short time earlier had been united by their opposition to the *vieux régime*. At the academic level, these divisions were manifested in the introduction of Marxism in the curriculum and the founding of the Université du Québec, in the radical non-Marxist critique of the North American way of life and its dominant ideology and assumptions, and in the increasing competition for academic positions. At the social level, these divisions were evident in the protests against bureaucratic planning, against the state as employer, against directive and integrative *animation sociale*, and in the radicalization of the nationalist movement.

The third period (1970–1986) covered by this study can be characterized as *legitimacy in crisis*. The profession continued to mature. New emphasis on the pursuit of doctoral studies in Quebec signalled an attempt to break the dependence of the social sciences on training outside the province; but this was only partially successful: More significant was the increased dependence of the profession on state funding. A downturn in the provincial economy led to increased pressure on provincial finances, including state spending on education, and to a reassessment of the role of the social sciences and of the returns on this social investment. With the exception of economics, the status of the social sciences as social technology had suffered from the protests that started in the mid-1960s and continued into the 1970s. There was also the fact of a shrinking job market in the provincial public sector for graduates of the social sciences. This contributed to the development of new language policies with a view to expanding job opportunities for francophones in the private sector.

This period also saw a continued politicization and fractiousness of popular groups during a time of relative scarcity. The initial solidarity of nationalist support for the Parti Québécois began to wither after the 1976 election as its referendum strategy forced the PQ to dilute its *in-dépendantiste* objectives and face the realities of governing. The great ambivalence of the CSN, the CEQ, and the leftist independentist groups expressed in their "critical Yes" position on sovereignty-association, indicated the growing difficulties encountered by the new middle class in its attempts to build class alliances and to maintain something more than a sullen acceptance of its political vehicle, the PQ, if only as the lesser evil or in the absence of an alternative.

The period covered by this study witnessed the downfall of one dominant ideology and its replacement by another more adequate to the society that Quebec had become. In this respect, it cannot be denied that social science intellectuals made a historic contribution to Quebec society. Admittedly, they were among the foremost beneficiaries of the transformation that is conventionally labelled the Quiet Revolution. Yet by integrating Quebec society into the North American intellectual mainstream they also confronted it with new problems and debates that were international in scope. The modernizing nationalism of the 1960s and 1970s, while grounded in Quebec history, was part of an international trend toward the assertion of nationalist demands. In the case of Quebec, social scientists succeeded all too well at the ideological level in pressing the case for national self-determination, given the inability of the new middle class to translate this into concrete political attainments and social unity.

The relationship of social scientists to politics in English Canada can be analyzed in terms of two roles which, though not mutually exclusive, have not overlapped to any considerable extent in practice. These are the roles of policy expert and social critic, the former oriented toward the state and the maintenance of social order, and the latter toward oppositional publics and challenge to that order. Social scientists, particularly economists, have achieved a high degree of integration as experts in the policy-making system, though their influence has arguably declined since the period of the Ottawa mandarinate in the 1950s. As social critics, the disengaged quiescence of the 1950s that John Porter remarked upon gave way before the nationalist and class analyses developed by sociology and political science during the 1960s. Within economics these critical perspectives were marginalized in the political economy tradition, surviving at the fringe of a profession which, under international influences, had evolved toward a paradigmatic consensus. Presumably, the roles of policy expert and social critic could come together in a reformist politics practised from within the state system. In Quebec, the roles of expert and critic temporarily achieved a measure of fusion through the ideological hegemony achieved in the alliance of nationalist social scientists with the ascendant new middle class. Opportunities for this sort of fusion have not developed in English Canada.

With the post-war adoption of Keynesian demand management policies involving (*inter alia*) a commitment to high and stable levels of employment, the Canadian state took a major step toward transforming itself into a capitalist welfare state. This marked the institutionalization of the special relationship of economics to public policy, and the bifurcation of the profession between the state and academe. Economists possessed technical skills and a comparatively high degree of paradigmatic consensus, buttressing the discipline's scientific claims and its perceived utility to the state in economic problem-solving. By comparison, the sociology and political science professions were focused principally on academe, with neither the level of theoretical consensus nor the technical sophistication that was evolving in economics. Opportunities for participation within the state were limited in any case. The implementation of major social programs and the development of linguistic equality into a leading political issue, policy areas in which non-economists could conceivably participate as experts, did not occur until the 1960s.

In examining the role of social scientists as critical leaven in the broader political system, it is difficult to determine what caused their general passivity. Was it due to a dearth of opportunities for such involvement? Or was it due to their own intellectual traditions while preoccupied with exchanging one colonial relationship (with Britain) for another (with the US)? Certainly the federal Liberal and Progressive Conservative parties, dominated by their parliamentary wings and assiduous practitioners of non-class politics, were unlikely instruments for the expression of critical ideas.[1] When the CCF was being recast as a party of urban industrial interests more representative of the society Canada had become in the thirty years since its founding, the conservative orientation of organized labour acted as a check on left-wing intellectuals within the party. Indeed, with rare exceptions like Eugene Forsey, the participation of intellectuals in labour organizations in English Canada was practically nil.

In response to increased university enrolment during the sixties, the social science community experienced rapid expansion. Much of the recruitment needed for the social sciences was met by American graduate schools, leading to stresses within the universities and ultimately to a nationalist reaction. A more important dimension of "Americanization," in political conflicts beyond the bounds of academe, was the extensive foreign control in the domestic economy and its consequences for industrial development and political sovereignty. As the contradictions of Canada's dependent economy were experienced more acutely in the form of truncated industrial development and the relatively small space for the expansion of indigenous capital outside of those sectors, like finance, traditionally dominated by domestic capital, the nationalist critique gained increasing force. Economic nationalism was reinforced by cultural nationalism, and by the opposition to American foreign policy in southeast Asia, to form a more general critique of what was viewed as US imperialism. This critique was not limited to left-leaning social scientists; it was given articulate expression both by Canada's philosopher of "red toryism," George Grant, and by the left-wing philosopher Charles Taylor, and was shared in by the radicalized student movement of the 1960s.

The emergence of critical currents within the social science community was not accompanied by the adequate development of the links with other sources of social criticism that would have been necessary to transform an academic critique into political praxis. Admittedly, the participation of social scientists in the NDP and the Committee for an Independent

Canada, their writings in periodicals like *Our Generation, Canadian Dimension,* and *Canadian Forum,* and their relationship to the student movement were manifestations of *engagement.* However, the influence on public policy that could be achieved through these channels was marginal.

The participation of social scientists as policy experts, integrated into the state or situated at its periphery through their involvement in royal commissions, government task forces, and independent advisory bodies, was consolidated during the 1960s. While this was particularly true for economists, the expansion of social programs and the research activities of the B and B Commission increased the opportunities for sociologists and political scientists to participate in the policy process. It is perhaps unnecessary to observe that integration into the policy process may not signify an increase in real influence. Critiques of social science expertise as "ideology," "political formula," and "justification" are plentiful; there is also an abundant literature on the failures of planning and rational policy-making systems.

In the Canadian case, the proliferation of contact points between the state and social science intellectuals mainly involved the further development of the special relationship of economics to public policy. Economics had evolved an orthodoxy–the neo-classical model–which had no serious challengers within the discipline. Consensus on the general assumptions underlying this model allowed economists to work at the tasks of problem-solving, measurement and technical elaboration of the model. Such work did not challenge the ideology of liberal capitalism through exploring its contradictions. The difference between orthodox economists and the growing corps of political economists in their analysis of the multinational corporation is illustrative of this point. Indeed, orthodox economists met the needs of the modern state for increasingly sophisticated techniques for measuring, forecasting, manipulating, and justifying economic activity.

The expert role of economists was reinforced during the 1970s with the expansion of policy analysis and evaluation functions within the federal state. In addition, the private sector of the economics community expanded with the creation of the C.D. Howe Institute and the Fraser Institute, and with the growth of the Conference Board. The influence of these organizations in the policy process is mainly indirect, through media coverage of, and political-bureaucratic elite attention to, the regular reports and forecasts and the special studies they produce, as well as through the informal network of personal and professional communications within the Canadian economics profession.

The orthodoxy of mainstream economics has been subject to growing criticism from various quarters over the past decade and a half, but hardly any fundamental doubts have been generated internally.[2] This degree of paradigmatic cohesion is quite unlike the condition of either sociology or political science, and contributes to the image of economics as the most scientific and, *ipso facto*, instrumentally useful of the social sciences in understanding and controlling social action in its area of competence.

The critical currents that emerged in political science and sociology during the 1960s have continued to evolve, primarily in the form of a new political economy which, unlike the Innisian tradition, employs an explicit class analysis in understanding society, public policy and the state. Moreover, the social criticism that developed around the Canadian nationalism issue in the 1960s has undergone a theoretical involution.[3] With the defeat of the Waffle movement in the NDP, nationalist intellectuals were deprived of a political vehicle for the wider dissemination of their analysis of Canada as a dependent society. Until fairly recently the link between left-wing intellectuals and the French communist party provided such a channel. A vehicle of this sort was necessary in order to move the nationalist critique beyond the relatively narrow confines of academe and establish it in social groups capable of political mobilization.

Over the past few years various oppositional publics have developed around the issues of equal rights for women, chronically high unemployment, and the "de-industrialization" of the Canadian economy, and the evident persistence of poverty among such socially marginal groups as native people, the aged, single mothers, and the working poor. A loose network of links has developed between some of the women's, church, and community organizations which have articulated these social criticisms, and left-wing social scientists working in the framework of the new political economy. The strategy pursued by these groups and allied intellectuals has focused on particular issues and policies: equal pay for work of equal value, free trade, and nuclear disarmament. Given the demonstrated resistance of Canada's party system and electoral politics to the mobilization of interests around these issues, alliances with community-level groups may well be the most effective forms of *engagement* for critical social scientists.

It is perhaps tempting to attribute the differences in the relationship of social scientists to politics in English Canada and French-speaking Quebec to cultural differences. There is, after all, a long tradition of viewing the politics of English Canada as relatively devoid of intellectuals and ideas. "Pragmatism" is the label that usually is applied to the politics of reconciling different regional and group interests through political parties whose policy platforms are largely determined by convenience rather than principle. This characterization of Canadian politics has seldom been better expressed than in F.R. Scott's satirical eulogy to the paragon of political pragmatism, Mackenzie King:

He seemed to be in the centre
Because we had no centre,
No vision
To pierce the smoke-screen of his politics.
Truly he will be remembered
Wherever men honour ingenuity,
Ambiguity, inactivity, and political longevity.
Let us raise up a temple
To the cult of mediocrity,
Do nothing by halves
Which can be done by quarters.[4]

French Canada, on the other hand, has never lacked intellectual spokespersons to articulate some vision of itself. The ideologists of French Canada until the period covered by this study were predominantly clerics, reflecting the social and political importance of the Catholic church in a society in which the development of strong secular elites had been stunted by the takeover of Montreal-based commerce by anglophones after the Conquest, and by the defeat of liberal political elements in Lower Canada in the 1837 Rebellion. Quebec's nationalist social scientists stepped easily into a tradition of *engagement* that had been established by clerics who found absurd the liberal notion of the separation of church and state and the associated idea that there existed some realm of "secular affairs" in which the church should not interfere. In conservative Quebec the clerics' tradition began visibly to crumble only in the middle of this century, at the time of the Asbestos Strike, when secular intellectuals enjoyed a prominence unparalleled in the rest of Canada. *Le Devoir*, the Institut canadien des affaires publiques, and the Ligue pour la défense du Canada were politically important organs for the journalists, writers, lawyers, and other non-clerics who actively participated in political discourse in the province.

To seek an explanation of these historical differences in the two cultures of French and English Canada is to miss the role of material factors in shaping politics, and the role of intellectuals in these interwoven societies. The crucial material difference is, of course, the economic and social subordination of French Canada after the Conquest. Conscious of this subordination, French-Canadian intellectuals, clerics and laymen alike, focused on *la nation française*; its attributes and the conditions for its survival were vital concerns from the standpoint of their social status. The conservative nationalism of *la survivance* was not simply a defense of the French language, the Catholic religion, and the values of *le peuple canadien*, but was also a justification of the social dominance of the clergy and its exponents in the liberal professions during the nineteenth and early twentieth centuries. The principal social institution in this conservative ideology was, of course, the church. It maintained solidarity in French Canada, while differentiating it from the rest of the country. Industrializing trends in Quebec would undermine the social authority of the church and the traditional elites by creating new conditions that cast increasing doubt on the relevance of the conservative ideology. The church in Quebec *did* attempt to manage these socio-economic changes, through Catholic trade unions, the social doctrine of corporatism, and church-controlled social institutions: schools, hospitals, and welfare agencies.[5] It was, however, from the social institutions run by the church that Quebec's new middle class of lay professionals emerged; after the secular reforms of the Quiet Revolution they would be among the main supporters and beneficiaries of the state-centred ideology of Québécois social scientists.

With the material basis of their social power and ideological authority eroded, the traditional intellectuals were vulnerable to challenges from those who articulated a conception of Quebec society expressing the ascendant interests of social groups created by the process of socioeconomic change. Nationalism, an ideology of exclusion, was not jettisoned by the intellectual spokespersons of the new Quebec; instead, they reworked both its basis and the social structures on which it depended. The basis of *la nation*, as expressed in the dominant interpretation of its history, changed from language and religion to language and socioeconomic dependency. The replacement of religion by dependency was crucial for two reasons. First, it meant that the clergy were discredited as ideologists of French Canada, and that secular intellectuals, including social scientists, became the chief interpreters of a history that was now understood in terms of economic dependency and social subordination instead of religion. Second, this new secularized version of French Canadian history, and more particularly of *les canadiens français du Québec*, cast an entirely different light on the future of *la nation* and its relationship to English Canada. The state, traditionally viewed as a second-class institution in a province where most social services were controlled by the church and government was associated with crass patronage, became the focus of nationalist energies.

That the new nationalism turned to the provincial state, in which French Canadians were unquestionably in the majority, reinforced the identification of French Canada with the territory of Quebec. The provincial Liberals' 1963 campaign slogan, "Maîtres chez nous," gave popular political expression to what among the province's francophone intellectuals had become the dominant view of French Canada as co-extensive with Quebec. The Quiet Revolution certainly was not brought about merely by the force of these new ideas. The economic and social changes that Quebec had been undergoing for decades had become irresistible, leaving vulnerable to political challenge the "unholy alliance" of the Union Nationale government, the church, and anglophone capital upon which *le vieux régime* rested. Thus, it was Quebec's unique pattern of socioeconomic development that provided the opportunity for the province's nationalist social scientists to play a historic role as the ideologists of the Quiet Revolution.

No such constellation of social and political developments emerged in English Canada. Unlike Quebec of the 1950s, English Canada was not confronted with a critical disjunction between its dominant ideology—liberalism—and the configuration of social and economic forces characterizing the society. The flawed nature of this society was exposed by John Porter and his successors. But the point is that the dominant ideology did not contradict modernizing tendencies within Canadian society; nor was it rejected by any politically influential segment of society, in the way that the conservative ideology of Duplessis and the traditional Quebec elite was rejected by those groups whose voice was *Cité libre*. Indeed, the failure to develop a viable alternative to the dominant ideology of liberalism, a failure linked to the disorganized character of the Canadian working class and to the incoherence of the nationalist position advocated by indigenous Canadian capital, was a factor in the defeat of the economic nationalism movement that developed in the 1960s.

The segment of Canadian capital represented by Walter Gordon and the nationalist wing of the Liberal Party was incapable of supporting Canadian nationalist social scientists in the way that Quebec's new middle class legitimated their francophone counterparts. The relative weakness of this interest was demonstrated in the Liberal government's ambivalence on both economic and cultural nationalism. Two task forces on foreign investment and the creation of the Canada Development Corporation (1971) were largely symbolic gestures; they were not matched by a political commitment to the measures prescribed by the nationalist critique. This was not surprising. The nationalism of indigenous capital was fundamentally incoherent; liberal thought could not square the internationalizing tendencies of modern capitalism with the state-protected hegemony of a local bourgeoisie. In this respect the "red Tory" George Grant, not the liberal Walter Gordon, was the more perceptive critic of the Canadian dilemma.

In the introduction to this study it was suggested that the very forces that have led to the explosive growth of the social sciences in this century, and to the integration of social scientists into the public policy process, have also resulted in the debasement of their intellectual function or, at least, a reduction in their capacity for social criticism. As the "markets" for the intellectual products created and disseminated by social scientists change, so too do the forms of intellectual activity. The social scientist as policy expert, as problem-solver, is called forth by the requirements of the modern capitalist state, and thus is an organic intellectual whose field of inquiry and enhanced status is tied to transformations in capitalist society.

The comparatively high level of technical sophistication characterizing contemporary economics and the peripheralization of dissent from its neo-classical paradigm have contributed to the integration of economists with the Canadian policy process, and, indeed to a phenomenon not found to any comparable degree in sociology or political science: the professional economist in the private sector, whose clients or employers may be either the state or private organizations. The ascendancy of the expert function has been at the expense of the traditional function of intellectuals as social critics. Obviously, economists frequently criticize the behaviour of governments or other agents in the economy. But they typically are *policy* critics, not *social* critics; their views do not challenge the basic premises of liberal capitalism.

This is not to suggest that the functions of expert and social critic necessarily are mutually exclusive. The case of Quebec during the Quiet Revolution, especially during the Lesage years of rapid state expansion and the secularization of social functions previously administered by the Catholic church, demonstrated that the roles could merge an ideological hegemony supplanting the previously dominant interests. In this instance the conceptualization of Quebec developed by francophone sociologists reinforced and legitimated the interests of the ascendant middle class, which required expansion of the provincial state and an assertive nationalism geared to modernization. At the same time, the Quebec-centred, statist nationalism of the 1960s enhanced the social significance of social scientists as a group, recalling Raymond Aron's explanation of why intellectuals tend to be more nationalistic than the general population: "[The intellectual] may believe himself to be indifferent to wealth or power, but he is never indifferent to national glory, for the scope and influence of his work partly depends on it."[6]

The exposition of social scientists' participation in the political process, either as experts linked to established power or as critics attached to oppositional groups, still leaves an unanswered question. Under what conditions are they influential? It has been argued that the particular conjunction of political and social developments that occurred during the Quiet Revolution promoted the ideological hegemony of Quebec's nationalist social scientists. It appears that the capacity to mobilize, or at least to legitimate the interests of an ascendant class or segment of a society's ruling elites, through the creation and dissemination of symbols and ideas that become social premises, is a precondition to this sort of ideological hegemony. Generalizations about the factors that determine *social receptivity* to the products of social scientists and other intellectuals would require many more cases and a longer historical period than are encompassed in the present study.

In this connection Samuel Eisenstadt has referred to the mode of institutionalization in which the ideas of intellectuals are transformed into the premises of society. He suggests that the process of interaction between intellectuals and ruling elites is a particularly important factor in a society's receptivity to the ideas and symbols generated by the former group.[7] Receptivity is not a simple function of the objective interests of a society's dominant groups, but is mediated by perception which attaches meaning to these interests. Thus, any attempt to develop generalizations in this area must go beyond an identification of the needs of the state and of social groups to the analysis of a constellation of the specific cultural, economic, and historical forces that determine the meaning attached to ideas. The ambitiousness of such an undertaking only serves to underline its importance to a fuller understanding of the relationship between social scientists and politics.

Notes

INTRODUCTION

1 T.S. Eliot, "On the Place and Function of the Clerisy," in *The Idea of a Christian Society and Other Writings* (London: Faber and Faber 1982), 159–167.

2 This is Marx's much-quoted eleventh thesis on Feuerbach. See David McLellan, ed., *Karl Marx: Selected Writings* (London: Oxford University Press 1977), 158.

3 Julien Benda, *The Treason of the Intellectuals* (New York: W.W. Norton and Co. 1969).

4 See Robert Brym, *Intellectuals and Politics* (London: George Allen and Unwin 1980), 12-13.

5 A. Turmel, "Universitaires et intellectuels," *Recherches sociographiques* 23, no. 3 (1982): 389.

6 Ibid., 400-1.

7 P. Bourdieu, J.C. Passeron, *La Reproduction* (Paris: Editions de Minuit 1970), 24. The "dominant arbitrary culture," according to these authors, is that of, and in the interests of, the dominant class or class fractions.

8 M. Lamont, "Le Pouvoir des intellectuels," *Politique*, 1, no. 1 (1982): 31.

9 A. Gramsci, *Selections from the Prison Notebooks* (New York: International Publishers 1971), 5-23.

10 Ibid., 12.

11 Bettina Aptheker, *The Academic Rebellion in the United States: A Marxist Approach* (Secaucus: Citadel Press 1972); Alain Touraine, *The May Movement: Revolt and Reform*, trans. L. Mayhew (New York: Random House 1971).

12 Brym, *Intellectuals and Politics*, 20.

13 See G.B. Rush et al., "Lament for a Notion: the Development of Social Science in Canada," *Canadian Review of Sociology and Anthropology* 18, no. 4 (1981): 519-44.

14 See the discussion in David L. Schalk, *The Spectrum of Political Engagement* (Princeton, N.J.: Princeton University Press 1979), 62.

15 Ibid., 65.

16 Barrington Moore, *The Social Origins of Dictatorship and Democracy* (Boston: Beacon Books 1966), 480.

17 S.M. Lipset and A. Basu, "The Roles of the Intellectual and Political Roles," in *The Intelligentsia and the Intellectuals*, ed. Aleksander Gella (Beverly Hills: Sage 1976), 129.

18 Ibid.

19 Raymond Aron, *The Opium of the Intellectuals* (New York: W. W. Norton and Co. 1962), 248.

20 Benda, *Treason of the Intellectuals*, 152.

21 Kenneth Boulding, *The Impact of the Social Sciences* (New Brunswick, N.J.: Rutgers University Press 1966), 6.

22 Ibid., 20.

23 See for example, J.J. Richardson, G. Gustasson and A.G. Jordan, "The Concept of Policy Style," in *Policy Styles in Western Europe*, ed. J.J. Richardson, (London: Allen and Unwin 1982).

24 Lipset and Basu, *"Roles of the Intellectual,"* 143.

25 See Carol Weiss, ed., *Using Social Research in Public Policy-Making* (Lexington, Mass.: D.C. Heath 1977), 16.

26 See I. Horowitz, "Social Science Mandarins: Policymaking as a Political Formula," *Policy Sciences* 1, no. 3 (1970): 339-60.

27 F. Knopfelmacher, *Intellectuals and Politics* (Melbourne: Nelson 1968), 13.

28 Alvin Gouldner, *The Coming Crisis of Western Sociology* (New York: Basic Books 1970). See p. 111 for Gouldner's distinction between academic and Marxist sociology.

29 Ibid., 156-7.

30 Ibid., 350.

31 Quoted in R. Scott and A. Shore, *Why Sociology Does Not Appy: A Study of the Use of Sociology in Public Policy* (New York: Elsevier 1979), 7.

32 Ibid., 13.

33 Hugh Hawkins, "The Ideal of Objectivity Among American Social Scientists in the Era of Professionalization, 1876–1916," in *Controversies and Decisions*, ed. C. Frankel, (New York: Russell Sage Foundation 1976): 89-102

34 Gouldner, *The Coming Crisis of Western Sociology*, 114.

35 Knopfelmacher, *Intellectuals and Politics*, 10.

36 Ibid., 8.

37 Ibid., 50.

38 See Norman and Jeanne MacKenzie, *The Fabians* (New York: Simon and Schuster 1977).

39 On the links between the LSR and the CCF see Michiel Horn, *The League for Social Reconstruction: Intellectual Origins of the Democratic Left in Canada, 1930–1942* (Toronto: University of Toronto Press 1980).

40 In his diaries King acknowledges the key role of Clark in shaping postwar fiscal policy. See also J. L. Granatstein, *The Ottawa Men: The Civil Service Mandarins 1935–1957* (Toronto: Oxford University Press, 1982), 44–61.

41 Quoted in Lipset and Basu, "Roles of the Intellectuals," 118.

42 Weiss, *Using Social Research*, 16.

43 Moore, *The Social Origins of Dictatorship and Democracy*, 480.

44 Adam Przeworski, *Capitalism and Social Democracy* (Cambridge: Cambridge University Press 1985), 101. For a discussion of the role of intellectuals in Canadian party politics see *Canadian Parties in Transition: Discourse, Organization and Representation*, ed. A.G. Gagnon and A. Brian Tanguay,(Toronto: Nelson, 1988).

45 Doug Owram, *The Government Generation: Canadian Intellectuals and the State 1900–1945* (Toronto: University of Toronto Press, 1986); J.L. Granatstein, *The Ottawa Men*; and Michiel Horn, *The League for Social Reconstruction*.

46 Marcel Fournier, *L'Entrée dans la modernité* (Montréal: Editions Saint-Martin 1986); and Douglas V. Verney, *Three Civilizations, Two Cultures, One State: Canada's Political Traditions* (Durham, N.C.: Duke University Press 1986).

CHAPTER ONE

1 See M.D. Behiels, *Prelude to Quebec's Quiet Revolution: Liberalism Versus Neo-Nationalism, 1945–1960* (Montréal: McGill-Queen's University Press 1985), 8–60.

2 Mgr L.A. Paquet, quoted in Yves Lamarche, "Position sociale des intellectuels et nationalisme: le cas de L'Action Française," in *Philosophie au Québec*, ed. C. Panaccio and P.A. Quintin, (Montréal: Bellarmin 1976), 156.

3 P.-A. Linteau, R. Durocher, J.-C. Robert, Quebec: A History 1867–1929 (Toronto: James Lorimer 1983). French Canadian capital remained insignificant well into the century, as is apparent from the data in Jacques Melançon, "Retard de croissance de l'entreprise canadienne-française," *L'Actualité Economique* (January–March, 1956): 503.

4 Marcel Fournier, "La Sociologie québécoise contemporaine," *Recherches sociographiques* 15, no. 2-3 (1974): 171; Paul Gervais, *Les Diplômés en sciences sociales dans la fonction publique du Québec* (Master's thesis, Université de Montréal 1979).

5 Peter Hopkins, *Daniel Johnson and the Quiet Revolution*, (Master's thesis, Simon Fraser University 1977) demonstrates this point very clearly.

6 See studies by Coleman, Bourque, Pelletier, Whitaker in A. G. Gagnon, ed., *Quebec: State and Society* (Toronto: Methuen 1984).

7 Marcel Fournier and Gilles Houle, "La Sociologie québécoise et son objet; problématique et débats," *Sociologie et sociétés* 12, no. 2 (1980): 28.

8 Ibid., 37.

9 J. Dofny and M. Rioux, "Les Classes sociales au Canada français," *Revue française de sociologie* 3, no. 3 (1962): 290-300.

10 Fournier and Houle, *La Sociologie québécoise*, 28.

11 Pierre Bourdieu and Jean-Claude Passeron, *La Reproduction* (Paris: Editions de Minuit 1970), 71. M. Fournier, "L'institutionnalisation des sciences sociales au Québec," *Sociologie et sociétés* 5, no. 1 (1973): 30.

12 J.-C. Saint-Armand, *L'Ecole sociale populaire et le syndicalisme catholique, 1911–1949* (Master's thesis, Laval University 1976) 1, in Raymond-G. Laliberté, "Dix-huit ans de corporatisme militant: l'Ecole sociale populaire de Montréal, 1933–1950," *Recherches sociographiques* 21, no. 1-2 (1980): 61.

13 J.-C. Falardeau coined this term in "Antécédents, débuts et croissance de la sociologie au Québec," *Recherches sociographiques* 15, no. 2-3 (1974).

14 Sister Marie-Agnès de Rome Gaudreau, *The Social Thought of French Canada as Reflected in the Semaines Sociales* (Washington: The Catholic University Press 1946), 239 in *La Grève de l'amiante*, ed. P.E. Trudeau, (Montréal: Editions du Jour 1970), 43.

15 R.-G. Laliberté, "Dix-huit ans de corporatisme," 68-71.

16 P.E. Trudeau, *La Grève de l'amiante*, 19-37.

17 R.-G. Laliberté, "Dix-huit ans de corporatisme," 82-91. See also Emile Bouvier, S.J., *L'Organisation corporative est-elle réalisable au Québec?* (Montréal: ISP no. 478, 1955), 23.

18 For a full account of Edouard Montpetit's contribution, see Marcel Fournier, "Edouard Montpetit et l'université moderne ou l'échec d'une génération," in *L'Entrée dans la modernité* (Montréal: Editions Saint-Martin 1986), 43-73.

19 M. Leclerc, *La Science politique au Québec* (Montréal: L'Hexagone 1982), 68.

20 Ibid., 71.

21 J.-C. Falardeau, "Antécédents," 143.

22 Data updated by Marcel Fournier. See *L'Entrée dans la modernité*, 72.

23 Ibid., 34.

24 Ibid., 34.

25 Ibid., 105.

26 Marcel Fournier "Sciences sociales, idéologie et pouvoir", *Possibles* 1, no. 1 (1976): 107.

27 M. Leclerc, *La Science politique au Québec*, 82. A. Anand, *A Sociological History of French-Canadian Sociology: Its Development at the Universities of Montreal and Laval* (Master's thesis, Carleton University 1973), 66.

28 Jean-Charles Falardeau, "Lettres à mes étudiants," *Cité libre* (May 1959), 8.

29 P. Garigue, "Avant-Propos," *Etudes sur le Canada français*, (Faculté des sciences sociales économiques et politiques, Université de Montréal 1958).

30 J.-C. Falardeau, "Antécédents," 146.

31 Cited in M. Fournier, "L'Institutionnalisation des sciences sociales au Québec," *Sociologie et sociétés* 5, no. 1 (1973): 43.

32 Ibid.

33 According to figures published in *The Labour Gazette* 49, no. 11(1949): 1384, the church provided a considerable support to the strike fund, collecting $167,558.24. See also S.H. Barnes, "Quebec Catholicism and Social Change," *The Review of Politics* 23, no. 1 (1961): 72-3.

34 Fournier, "L'Institutionnalisation," 46.

35 The issue of confessionality is fully discussed in P.M. Gaudrault, O.P., *Neutralité, non-confessionnalité et l'Ecole sociale populaire* (Montréal: Levrier 1946).

36 René Lévesque, *Attendez que je me rappelle ...* (Montréal: Québec/Amérique 1986), 201-7.

37 Albert Breton et al., "An Appeal for Realism in Politics," *Canadian Forum* (May 1964): 29, 32.

38 Fournier, "L'institutionnalisation," 44.

39 Fournier, "L'institutionnalisation," 50. In 1950–51, federal grants constituted 13 per cent of University revenues.

40 Jean-Charles Falardeau, "Les octrois fédéraux aux universités," *Le Devoir* (23 October 1956): 4.

41 Léon Dion, "Aspects de la condition du professeur d'université dans la société canadienne-française," *Cité libre* 26 (July 1958): 23.

42 Pierre Elliott Trudeau, *Federalism and the French Canadians* (Toronto: Macmillan 1968), 79–102. See also M.D. Behiels, *Prelude to Quebec's Quiet Revolution*, 206-11.

43 M. Leclerc, *La science politique au Québec*, 84-5, 112; A. Anand, *A Sociological History*, 122-30.

CHAPTER TWO

1 Marcel Fournier developed a similar position in "Les conflits de discipline: philosophie et sciences sociales," in *Philosophie au Québec*, ed. C. Panaccio and Paul-André Quintin (Montréal: Bellarmin 1976), 207-236.

2 M. Leclerc, *La Science politique au Québec* (Montréal: Hexagone 1982), 193; M. Fournier and L. Maheu, "Nationalismes et nationalisation du champ scientifique québécois," *Sociologie et sociétés* 7, no. 2 (1975): 100.

3 M. Leclerc, *La Science politique au Québec*, 199.

4 Ibid., 202.

5 M. Fournier, L. Maheu, "Nationalismes et nationalisation," 100.

6 For a historical account, see Alain Gagnon, "L'Influence de l'Eglise sur l'évolution socio-économique du Québec, 1850–1950," *L'Action nationale* 49, no.4 (1979): 252-77.

7 See Léon Dion, *Le Bill 60 et la société québécoise* (Montréal: HMH 1967).

8 Don Murray and Vera Murray, *De Bourassa à Lévesque* (Montréal: Editions Quinze 1978) 57-9.

9 This notion of a "party of intellectuals" is developed by Maurice Pinard and Richard Hamilton, "The Leadership Roles of Intellectuals in Party Politics" (unpublished paper, 1987).

10 F. Dumont, J.-C. Falardeau "Pour la recherche sociographique du Canada français," *Recherches sociographiques* 1, no. 1 (1960): 3-5.

11 J. Dofny, "Editorial," *Sociologie et sociétés* 1, no. 1 (1969): 3-6.

12 See M. Renaud, "Quebec New Middle Class in Search of Social Hegemony," in *Quebec: State and Society*, ed. A.G. Gagnon (Toronto: Methuen 1984) 148-185: D. Brunelle, *La désillusion tranquille* (Montréal: Editions Hurtubise 1979), 45–84; and J.-J. Simard, "La Longue Marche des technocrates," *Recherches sociographiques* 18, no. 1 (January-April, 1977): 115-29.

13 J.-J. Simard, "La Longue Marche," M. Fournier, "Sciences sociales, idéologie et pouvoir," *Possibles* 1, no. 1 (1976): 99-110; A Anand, *A Sociological History of French-Canadian Sociology*, 122-89.

14 See Charles Taylor, "Nationalism and the Political Intelligentsia: A Case Study," *Queen's Quarterly* (Spring 1965); K. McRoberts and D. Posgate, *Quebec: Social Change and Political Crisis* (Toronto: McClelland and Stewart 1980).

15 M. Fournier, "L'Institutionnalisation des sciences sociales au Québec," *Sociologie et sociétés* 5, no. 1 (May 1973): 53-4.

16 J.-J. Simard, "La Longue Marche," 116-17.

17 Marc Renaud, "Québec New Middle Class," 155-6.

18 Fournier, *L'Entrée dans la modernité* (Montréal: Editions Saint-Martin 1986), 158-9.

19 Philippe Garigue, "French Canada: A Case Study in Sociological Analysis," *Canadian Review of Sociology and Anthropology* 1, no. 4 (November 1964): 191.

20 For some historical and analytical perspectives on particular social sciences, see the numerous essays collected in *Continuité et rupture: Les sciences sociales au Québec*, 2 vols. (Montréal: PUM 1984). For the intellectual itineraries of some of Québec's most eminent sociologists, see the collection of "Itinéraires sociologiques," in *La Sociologie au Québec: Recherches Sociographiques* 15, no. 2-3 (May-August 1974): 201-312. For a study of political science, see M. Leclerc, *La Science politique au Québec* (Montréal: L'Hexagone 1982). For an intellectual biography of one of Quebec's most famous sociologists, see J. Duchastel, *Marcel Rioux: Entre l'utopie et la raison* (Montréal: Nouvelle Optique 1981).

21 M. Fournier and L. Maheu, "Nationalismes et nationalisation du champ scientifique québécois," *Sociologie et sociétés*, 7, no. 2 (1975): 100-9.

22 Gouvernement du Québec, *La Politique québécoise du développement culturel*, Livre blanc, vol. 2 (Editeur officiel du Québec 1978), 283.

23 M.D. Behiels, "Quebec: Social Transformation and Ideological Renewal, 1940–1976," in *Modern Canada, 1930–1980's: Readings in Social History*, ed. M.S. Cross and G.S. Kealey (Toronto: McClelland and Stewart 1984), vol. 5, 166–

71. See also M. Séguin, *La Nation canadienne et l'agriculture 1760–1850* (Trois-Rivières: Boréal Express 1970); and M. Brunet, *French Canada in the Early Decades of British Rule, 1760–1791* (Ottawa: Canadian Historical Association Pamphlet 13, 1963).

24 M. Fournier and G. Houle, "La Sociologie québécoise et son objet: problématiques et débats," *Sociologie et sociétés* 12, no. 2 (1980): 29-35.

25 Ibid., 34-5.

26 A useful account is provided in D.V. Verney, *Three Civilizations, Two Cultures, One State: Canada's Political Traditions* (Durham: Duke University Press 1986) 58-111. See also Fournier and Houle, *La Sociologie québécoise*, 42-3. See also D. Nock, "History and Evolution of Canadian Sociology," *The Insurgent Sociologist* 4, no. 4 (1974): 25; J. Harp and J.E. Curtis, "Linguistic Communities and Sociology: Data from the Canadian Case," in *Social Process and Institution: The Canadian Case* ed. James E. Gallagher and Ronald D. Lambert (Toronto: Holt, Rinehart and Winston 1971) 57-71; and D. Whyte, "Sociology and the Nationalist Challenge in Canada," *Journal of Canadian Studies* 19, no. 4 (Winter 1984-5): 106-29.

27 In terms of funding, it should be indicated here that in 1967–8, for instance, out of the $25.5 million provided to Quebec universities as subsidies, only $2.2 million (8.5%) came from American sources. Since then, this percentage fell to 4.5% in 1969–70, but rose to 5.1% in 1980–81 ($6 million). Approximately 40% of these funds support medical research. See *Les Principes de la politique scientifique du Québec* (Québec: Ministère de l'Education, Comité des politiques scientifiques du Québec 1971); *Les Subventions et contrats de recherche des universités du Québec en 1979–80 et 1980–81* (Québec: Ministère de l'éducation, direction générale de l'enseignement et de la recherche universitaire 1983).

28 Fernand Dumont and Yves Martin, eds., *Situation de la recherche sur le Canada français* (Québec: Presses de l'Université Laval 1963). For a more recent account, see the contributions by Gérald Fortin, Louis Maheu, Jacques Godbout, and Jean-Jacques Simard in L'Association canadienne des sociologues et anthropologues de langue française, *La Transformation du pouvoir au Québec* (Montréal: Editions Albert St. Martin 1980).

29 Fernand Dumont, "Le sociologue et le pouvoir," in *Le Pouvoir dans la société canadienne-française* ed. F. Dumont and J.-P Montminy, (Québec: Presses de l'Université Laval 1966), 11-20.

30 See Ramsay Cook, "Au Diable avec le Goupillon et la Tuque: the Quiet Revolution and the New Nationalism," in *Canada, Quebec and the Uses of Nationalism* (Toronto: McClelland and Stewart 1986), 68-86.

31 Anand, *A Sociological History*, 144-65.

32 These experiences of development have been discussed in J.-J. Simard, *La Longue Marche*, 75-113. See also A.G. Gagnon, *Développement régional, état et groupes populaires* (Hull: Asticou 1985) 119-162.

33 Simard, *La Longue marche*, 141, 143-4.

34 Ibid., 120-9.
35 G. Gagnon, "Sociologie, mouvements sociaux, conduites de rupture: le cas québécois," *Sociologie et sociétés* 10, no. 2 (1978): 117.
36 J.-J. Simard, *La Longue Marche des technocrates*, 54-71.
37 A.G. Gagnon, *Développement régional*, 183-208.
38 P. Hamel, J.-F. Léonard, and R. Mayer, *Les Mobilisations populaires urbaines* (Montréal: Nouvelle Optique 1982); H. Lamoureux, R. Mayer, and J. Panet-Raymond, *L'Intervention communautaire* (Montréal: Editions Saint-Martin 1984).
39 M. Corbeil, "Historique de l'animation sociale au Québec," *Relations* no. 349 (1970): 142.
40 L.M. Tremblay, *Le Syndicalisme québécois–idéologies de la* CSN et de la FTQ (1940–1970) (Montréal: PUM 1972), 43.
41 *Ibid.*, 45, referring to S. Perlman, *A Theory of the Labour Movement* (New York: Augustus M. Kelley 1966).
42 Black Rose Books Collective, *Quebec Labour: The Confederation of National Trade Unions Yesterday and Today* (Montreal: Black Rose Books and Our Generation Press 1972).
43 Roch Denis, *Luttes de classe et question nationale du Québec: 1948–1968* (Montréal-Paris: Presses socialistes internationales 1979), 360.
44 Ibid., 363.
45 Ibid., 381, quoting from "Manifeste 1964–65," *Parti pris* 2, no. 1 (1964): 14.
46 Ibid., 472, quoting from "Manifeste 1965–66," *Parti pris* 3, no. 1-2 (1965): 24.
47 André J. Bélanger has provided an important contribution on this period in *Ruptures et constantes: Quatre idéologies du Québec en éclatement, la Relève, la JEC, Cité libre, Parti pris* (Montréal: Hurtubise HMH 1977).

CHAPTER THREE

1 Pierre Elliott Trudeau, Official Text of the Prime Minister's Speech at the Liberal Party of Canada (Québec) Fund Raising Luncheon in Montreal, 30 November 1980. Michèle Lalonde, Hélène Pelletier-Baillargeon, Paul Chamberland, Denis Monière, "Des intellectuels et artistes répondent à Trudeau," *Le Devoir*, 11 December 1980. A series of articles were published in *Le Devoir* as the exchange between the Prime Minister and these intellectuals became acerbic. See P.E. Trudeau, "Réponse à un groupe d'intellectuels du Québec," *Le Devoir*, 31 December 1980; and M. Lalonde, P. Chamberland, D. Monière, H. Pelletier-Baillargeon, "M. Trudeau et les intellectuels québécois," *Le Devoir*, 13-14 January 1981.
2 Jean-Charles Falardeau, "Antécédents, débuts et croissance de la sociologie au Québec," *Recherches sociographiques*, 15, no. 2-3 (1974): 162-3. G. Bourque and J. Duchastel, "L'UQAM et la gauche," *Les Cahiers du Socialisme*, 7 (1981): 10-21.

3 Anne Legaré, "The Times and Promises of a Debate: Class Analyses in Quebec (1960–1980)," in A.G. Gagnon, ed., *Quebec: State and Society*, (Toronto: Methuen 1984), 92-112; R. Vandycke, "La question nationale: Où en est la pensée marxiste," *Recherches sociographiques*, 21, no. 1-2, (January-August 1980): 97-129; Anne Legaré, *Les Classes sociales au Québec* (Montréal: Presses de l'Université du Québec 1977), 119-177.

4 See the debates in A.G. Gagnon, *Quebec: State and Society*, 124-227. This question is also discussed in G. Boismenu et al., *Espace régional et nation: Pour un nouveau débat sur le Québec* (Montréal: Boréal Express 1983), 119-155.

5 A recent study by S. Proulx and P. Vallières, *Changer de société: Déclin du nationalisme, crise culturelle, alternatives sociales au Québec* (Montréal: Québec/Amérique 1982) clearly demonstrates this point.

6 M. Fournier, "Le CFP et le mouvement ouvrier: Une expérience de formation," *Possibles*, 3, no. 2 (1979): 41.

7 Ibid., 40, quoting from "Le CFP et le mouvement ouvrier," *Bulletin de Liaison du CFP* 1, no. 4 (1978): 2-3.

8 For a discussion of PQ labour legislation, see A.G. Gagnon and M.-B. Montcalm, "The Global Economic Crisis and Québec's Peripheral Position in the Capitalist Economy," in *Frontyard/Backyard: The Americas in the Global Crisis*, ed. J. Holmes and C. Leys (Toronto: Between the lines 1987), 131-47.

9 M. Fournier, "Le CFP et le mouvement ouvrier," 40.

10 Ibid. For a critique of *autogestion* thought from a social-democratic perspective see G. Durand, "Des porteurs de stylos aux porteurs d'utopie," *Possibles* 7, no. 2 (1983): 27-37.

11 See Marcel Rioux's introductory editorial, "Les possibles dans une période de transition," *Possibles* 1, no. 1 (1976): 3-8.

12 G. Bourque and J. Duchastel, "L'UQAM et la gauche," *Les Cahiers du socialisme* 8 (1981): 10-21.

13 Michel Freitag, "Pourquoi ces Cahiers," *Cahiers de recherche sociologique* 1 (September 1983): 4.

14 Denis Monière, "Présentation," *Politique* 1, no. 1 (January 1982): 6.

15 Claude Martin and Marc-Henry Soulet, "L'Hiver québécois des sociologues et des travailleurs sociaux ...," *Economie et humanisme* 281 (January-February 1985): 87-95. *Possibles* devotes an entire issue to this important question; see "Du côté des intellectuel(le)s," *Possibles* 10, no. 2 (Winter 1986).

16 See A.G. Gagnon, "Intercommunal Relations and Language Policy in Québec, 1960–1986," in *Social Issues: Sociological Views of Canada*, ed. D. Forcese and S. Richer (Scarborough: Prentice-Hall, 1988), 83–96.

17 Gilles Paquet, "Entrepreneurship canadien-français: Mythes et réalités." (Paper presented at the Colloquium of the Royal Society of Canada on Francophones in Canada, University of Manitoba, 3 July 1986), 30.

18 See the reports on these conferences in *La Presse*, 8 November 1983, A7; 8 February 1984, A5; 11 February 1984, A7; *Le Devoir*, 8 February 1984, 2; *Le Soleil*, 9 February 1984; A1; and *The Gazette*, 13 February 1984, A3.

19 Thomas J. Courchene, "Market Nationalism," *Policy Options* (October 1986): 11.

20 See, for example, *Le Québec dans le monde ou le défi de l'interdépendance: Enoncé de politique de relations internationales* (Québec: Ministère des relations internationales, June 1985).

21 Rapport final du groupe de travail sur la déréglementation, *Réglementer moins et mieux* (Québec: Gouvernement du Québec 1986); Groupe de travail sur la révision des fonctions et des organissations gouvernementales, *L'Organisation gouvernementale* (Québec: Gouvernement du Québec 1986); and Rapport du comité sur la privatisation des sociétés d'Etat, *De la révolution tranquille ... à l'an deux mille* (Québec: Gouvernement du Québec 1986).

22 R.D. French, "La crise d'une hégémonie," *Le Devoir*, 16 December 1982, 7.

23 G. Lesage, "Plus qu'un débat entre Québec et Ottawa, une polarisation entre deux bourgeoisies," interview with Richard French, *Le Devoir* 28 June 1984, 2.

24 Yvon Laberge, "Bourassa change le rôle de l'Etat," *La Presse*, 13 December 1985, A1-2.

25 See Alain G. Gagnon and Khayyam Z. Paltiel, "Toward Maîtres Chez Nous: The Ascendancy of a Balzacian Bourgeoisie in Quebec," *Queen's Quarterly* 93, no. 4 (Winter 1986): 731-49.

26 Jacques Parizeau, quoted in "Much to Celebrate as HEC marks 75th year," *The Gazette*, 27 August, 1985, B5.

27 N. Provencher, "Third of all MBA's to graduate from Québec schools," *The Gazette*, 23 February 1985, C1.

28 Ibid.

29 J. Steed, "The Unquiet Revolution," *Report on Business Magazine* (May 1985): 19.

30 Lawrence Martin, "New Francophone Business Class Booming," *The Globe and Mail*, 16 February 1985, 8; N. Provencher, "The Young Turks Take Over," *The Gazette*, 23 February 1985, C1.

31 A. Wilson-Smith and B. Wallace, "Quebec's New Entrepreneurs," *Maclean's* (4 August, 1986): 25.

32 *L'organisation gouvernementale*, 16.

33 Claude Martin, Marc-Henry Soulet, "L'Hiver québécois des sociologues et des travailleurs sociaux ... une anticipation pour la France?," *Economie et Humanisme*, no. 281 (January–February 1985): 90.

34 Jean Royer, "Le Oui des écrivains," *Le Devoir*, 17 May 1980, 21; J. Dufresne, "Où en sont les intellectuels?," *Le Devoir*, 4 February 1982, 15.

CHAPTER FOUR

1 See "The Social Sciences," in Julian Park, ed., *The Culture of Contemporary Canada* (Ithaca, New York: Cornell University Press 1957), 181-221; and especially "After Strange Gods: Canadian Political 1973," in *Perspectives on the Social Sciences in Canada*, ed. T.N. Guinsberg and G.L. Reuber, (Toronto: University of Toronto Press 1974), 52-76.

2 John Porter, *The Vertical Mosaic* (Toronto: University of Toronto Press 1965), 491-507.

3 See Donald Whyte, "Sociology and the Nationalist Challenge," *Journal of Canadian Studies* 19, no. 4 (Winter 1984—5), 106-29; and G.B. Rush et al., "Lament for a Notion: the Development of Social Science in Canada," *Canadian Review of Sociology and Anthropology* 18 no. 4 (1981): 519-44.

4 Two notable exceptions are Doug Owram's masterful study, *The Government Generation: Canadian Intellectuals and the State 1900–1945* (Toronto: University of Toronto Press 1986), which leaves off roughly where the present study begins, and J.L. Granatstein's, *The Ottawa Men: The Civil Service Mandarins 1935–1957* (Toronto: Oxford University Press 1982), which focuses more narrowly and intensely on the participation of intellectuals in the federal bureaucracy than does our analysis.

5 John Porter, *The Vertical Mosaic*, 504.

6 This is not to imply either that the political economy approach originated in Canada, or that scholars elsewhere did not work within this framework.

7 C.B. Macpherson, "The Social Sciences," in *The Culture of Contemporary Canada*, 190.

8 See Michel Brunet, "The British Conquest: Canadian Social Scientists and the Fate of the Canadiens", in *Approaches to Canadian History*, ed. Carl Berger, (Toronto: University of Toronto Press 1979), 84-98.

9 On the zenith and subsequent decline of the Ottawa mandarinate see J.L. Granatstein, *The Ottawa Men* (Toronto: Oxford University Press 1982).

10 Quoted in Carl Berger, *The Writing of Canadian History*, 2nd ed. (Toronto: University of Toronto Press 1986), 24.

11 Ibid., 52

12 Donald Creighton, *Harold Adams Innis: Portrait of a Scholar* (Toronto: University of Toronto Press 1957), 81-94.

13 Berger, *The Writing of Canadian History*, 101.

14 See Innis' article, "The Rowell-Sirois Report," *Canadian Journal of Economics and Political Science* 5, no. 4 (November 1940): 563-4.

15 Exceptions to this generalization include C.B. Macpherson, *Democracy in Alberta: The Theory and Practice of a Quasi-Party System* (Toronto: University of Toronto Press 1953); and, much less explicitly, J.R. Mallory, *Social Credit and the Federal Power in Canada* (Toronto: University of Toronto Press 1955).

16 R.M. Dawson, *The Government of Canada* (Toronto: University of Toronto Press 1947).

17 D. Smiley, "Contributions to Canadian Political Science Since the Second World War," *Canadian Journal of Economics and Polical Science* 33, no. 4 (November 1967): 576.

18 Anthony Scott, "The Recruitment and Migration of Canadian Social Scientists," *Canadian Journal of Economics and Polical Science* 32, no. 4 (November 1967): 498 (note 4).

19 *Ibid.*, 496-8.

20 See Porter, *The Vertical Mosaic*, 611 for an explanation of how the deputy-ministerial level was operationalized.

21 Quoted in Porter, *The Vertical Mosaic*, 435.

22 See D.A. MacGibbon, "Economics and the Social Order", *Canadian Journal of Economics and Polical Science* 2, no. 1 (February 1936); and the discussion of the intellectual climate of Canadian economics in the 1930s in Doug Owram, *The Government Generation*, 192-220.

23 The reader should be aware that the term "intelligentsia" is neither in its origins nor in its common use meant to refer to intellectual experts. What King refered to as the intelligentsia was more aptly called the "brain trust" in the United States during Roosevelt's New Deal.

24 Quoted in Owram, *The Government Generation*, 316-17.

25 This assessment follows S.D. Clark's account in "The Changing Image of Sociology in English-speaking Canada," *Canadian Journal of Sociology* 4, no. 4 (1979): 393-403.

26 Ibid., 398-9.

27 Regarding the relative prestige of the two disciplines, it is sufficient to observe that political science could claim no Keynes, associated with a model on which there was a high degree of professional consensus.

28 Donald Smiley makes this point when he argues: "The dissolution of the professional relation between economists and political scientists can only work toward ratifying and legitimizing the position of the former as the authoritative academic specialists in respect to these matters." ("Contributions to Canadian Political Science," 570.)

29 See Jean Leca, "La Science politique dans le champ intellectuel français," *Revue française de science politique* 32, nos. 4-5 (August-October 1982), 653-78.

30 Institutionalization here is meant to refer to the process whereby the political science community became increasingly autonomous, eventually achieving its own professional association, journal and organizational trappings.

31 Thomas S. Kuhn writes: "Close historical investigation of a given specialty at a given time discloses a set of recurrent and quasi-standard illustrations of various theories in their conceptual, observational, and instrumental applications. These are the community's paradigms, revealed in its textbooks, lectures, and laboratory exercises ... Despite occasional ambiguities, the par-

adigms of a mature scientific community can be determined with relative ease." *The Structure of Scientific Revolutions*, 2nd ed. (Chicago: University of Chicago Press 1970), 43.

32 Donald Whyte, "Sociology and the Nationalist Challenge," *Journal of Canadian Studies* 19, no. 4 (Winter 1984–5): 116.

33 See André Gunder Frank, *Capitalism and Under-Development in Latin America* (London: Monthly Review Press 1969).

34 Reginald Whitaker, *The Government Party: Organizing and Financing the Liberal Party of Canada, 1930–58* (Toronto: University of Toronto Press 1979), 411.

35 See Walter D. Young, *Anatomy of a Party: The National CCF, 1932–1961* (Toronto: University of Toronto Press 1969).

36 Seymour Martin Lipset, *Agrarian Socialism* (Los Angeles: University of California Press 1950), ch. 12

37 For positive assessments see the chapters by George Cadbury and Meyer Brownstone in *Essays on the Left*, ed. Laurier Lapierre (Toronto: McClelland and Stewart 1971). Pratt and Richards, *Prairie Capitalism* (Toronto: McClelland and Stewart 1981), 139-44, and S.M. Lipset, *Agrarian Socialism*, ch. 12, provide more critical assessments.

38 See League for Social Reconstruction, *Social Planning for Canada* (Toronto: University of Toronto Press 1975).

CHAPTER FIVE

1 H. Johnson, "The current and prospective state of economics in Canada," in *Perspectives on the Social Sciences in Canada*, ed. T.N. Guinsberg and G.L. Reuber (Toronto: University of Toronto Press 1974), 119.

2 Ibid., 104. See also Johnson's comments on C.B. Macpherson's paper, 79-84

3 Ibid., 86.

4 See R. March and R. Jackson, "Aspects of the State of Political Science in Canada," *Midwest Journal of Political Science* 11, no. 4 (November, 1967): 433-50.

5 Johnson, quoted in "Schools Brief: Economics Ancient and Modern," *The Economist*, 22 September 1984, 49.

6 See Christian Bay, "Politics and Pseudopolitics: A Critical Evaluation of Some Behavioral Literature," *American Political Science Review* 59, no. 1 (March 1965), 39-51.

7 René Hurtubise and Donald Rowat, *The University, Society and Government* (Ottawa: University of Ottawa Press 1970), 175.

8 These figures are taken from the Science Council of Canada, *The Role of Federal Government Support of Research in Canadian Universities* (Ottawa: Queen's Printer 1969), 78, table 4: 3; and Social Sciences and Humanities Research Council of Canada, *Five-Year Plan for Financing Research in the Social Sciences and*

Humanities, 1985–1990 (Ottawa: Minister of Supply and Services 1985), 38, fig. 5.

9 Private foundations in Canada, such as the Donner Foundation and the C.D. Howe Memorial Foundation, were insignificant sources of funding compared to their counterparts in the United States.

10 For a detailed description of the vast body of unpublished research undertaken for the B and B Commission, see Christopher R. Adamson et. al., "The Unpublished Research of the Royal Commission on Bilingualism and Biculturalism," *Canadian Journal of Political Science* 7, no. 4 (December 1974): 709-20.

11 Porter, *The Vertical Mosaic*, 368-9.

12 Ian Adams et al., *The Real Poverty Report* (Edmonton: M.G. Hurtig 1971), v. The four Special Senate Committee on Poverty staff members who produced the study resigned their positions when, in their words, "it had become quite apparent to the four of us that the Senate committee was not going to live up to its mandate. Any attempt to discuss the actual production of poverty in Canada ... was systematically eliminated from the drafts of the report."

13 See M. Prince and J. Chenier, "The Rise and Fall of Policy Planning and Research Units: An Organizational Perspective," *Canadian Public Administration* 23 no. 4 (Winter 1980): 526-7.

14 See Arthur Smith, "The Economic Council of Canada," in *Economic Policy Advising in Canada*, ed. D.C. Smith (Montreal: C.D. Howe Institute 1984), 80.

15 G.B. Doern, "The Science Council of Canada," in *The Structure of Policy-Making in Canada*, ed. G.B. Doern and P. Aucoin (Toronto: Macmillan 1971), 259-60.

16 This thesis is developed in G.B. Rush et al., "Lament for a Notion: the Development of Social Science in Canada," *Canadian Review of Sociology and Anthropology* 18, no. 4 (1981): 519-44.

17 Grant's main writings on this subject are *Lament for a Nation* (Toronto: McClelland and Stewart 1965), and *Technology and Empire* (Toronto: Anansi 1969).

18 See Robin Matthews and James Steele, eds., *The Struggle for Canadian Universities* (Toronto 1969). For other positions in this debate see Canadian Association of University Teachers, "Canadianization and the University," *Bulletin* 22, no. 3 (January 1974).

19 See H.C. Eastman and S. Stykolt, *The Tariff and Competition in Canada* (Toronto: Macmillan 1967); and H.E. English, *Industrial Structure in Canada's International Competitive Position* (Montreal: Canadian Trade Committee 1964).

20 See Stephen Brooks, "Direct Investment by the State: Mixed Enterprise in Canada" (unpublished PHD thesis Carleton University, Ottawa 1985), 74-82.

21 See Kari Levitt, *Silent Surrender: The Multinational Corporation in Canada* (Toronto: Macmillan 1970); Charles Taylor, *The Pattern of Politics* (Toronto: McClelland and Stewart 1970); R.M. Laxer, ed., *(Canada) Ltd.: The Political Economy of Dependency* (Toronto: McClelland and Stewart 1973); A. Rotstein and G. Lax, eds., *Independence: The Canadian Challenge* (Toronto: Committee for an Independent Canada 1972).

22 See Canada, Privy Council Office, Report of the Task Force on the Structure of Canadian Industry, *Foreign Ownership and the Structure of Canadian Industry* (Ottawa: Queen's Printer 1968); Canada, *Report on the Task Force on Foreign Direct Investment in Canada* (Ottawa: Queen's Printer 1972); Ontario, *Report of the Select Committee on Economic and Cultural Nationalism* (Toronto: Queen's Printer 1975).

23 On the revitalization of political economy in Canada see Michael Stein and John Trent, "Canada," in *The International Handbook of Political Science* (Westport: Greenwood Press 1982), 121-2; and Reginald Whitaker, "Confused Alarms of Struggle and Flight: English-Canadian Political Science in the 1970s," *Canadian Historical Review* 50, no. 1 (1979): 16-17.

24 Whyte, "Sociology and the Nationalist Challenge," 121.

25 See for example, Phil Resnick, "Towards a Class Analysis of Canada," *Papers Presented to the 44th Annual Meeting of the* CPSA (Montreal, 1972); and Michael Gurstein, "Towards the Nationalization of Canadian Sociology," *Journal of Canadian Studies* 7, no. 3 (August 1972): 50-8.

26 Alan Cairns "Political Science in Canada and the Americanization Issue," *Canadian Journal of Political Science* 8, no. 2 (June 1975): 212.

27 This was the view of most of the academics who wrote on the issue in Canadian Association of University Teachers, "Canadianization and the University," as well as being the official position of CAUT.

28 Canada, *Report of the Royal Commission on Dominion-Provincial Relations*, 3 vols. (Ottawa: Queen's Printer 1940).

29 Although Gordon's nationalism was viewed positively by many social scientists on the left, it is clear that he did not envisage any fundamental change in the capitalist economy. Gordon wished merely to substitute Canadian managers and owners for non-Canadians.

30 Paul Samuelson, *Economics*, International Student Edition, 8th ed. (New York: McGraw-Hill Kogakusha 1970).

31 R. Lipsey and P.O. Steiner, *Economics*, 2nd ed. (New York: Harper and Row 1969).

32 Stephen Clarkson has developed this argument at considerable length in "Anti-Nationalism in Canada: The Ideology of Mainstream Economics" *Canadian Review of Studies in Nationalism* 5, no. 1 (Spring 1978): 45-65.

33 See Gad Horowitz, "Creative Politics Mosaic and Identity," *Canadian Dimension* 3, no. 1 (Nov.-Dec. 1965): 14-15, 28; and 3, no. 2 (Jan.-Feb. 1966): 17-19.

CHAPTER SIX

1 Kari Levitt, "Towards decolonization: Canada and Quebec," *Canadian Forum* (March 1972): 3.
2 Michael Cross, "Third Class on the Titanic: The NDP Convention," *Canadian Forum* (April-May 1971): 5.
3 Ibid., 4.
4 For an example of this argument see Patricia Marchak, *Ideological Perspectives on Canada* (Toronto: McGraw-Hill Ryerson 1975).
5 See Pierre Trudeau, "Quebec on the Eve of the Asbestos Strike," in *French Canadian Nationalism*, ed. R. Cook (Toronto: Macmillan 1969), 32-48.
6 See Richard French, *How Ottawa Decides: Planning and Industrial Policy-Making 1968-1980* (Toronto: Lorimer 1983), ch. 2.
7 Donald Whyte, "Sociology and the Nationalist Challenge," *Journal of Canadian Studies* 19, no. 4 (Winter 1984–5): 125 (footnote 23).
8 Ibid. Unfortunately, Whyte provides neither a citation nor details of the study to which he refers.
9 David Smith, ed., *Economic Policy Advising in Canada* (Montreal: C.D. Howe Institute 1981).
10 The Fraser Institute's objectives are set forth in a statement which appears on the inside covers of its publications.
11 See the statement of the IRPP's goals which appears in the monographs it publishes.
12 See Evert A. Lindquist, "Policy Institutes in Canada: Looking Westward," *American Review of Canadian Studies* 16, no. 3: 327-40.
13 While we have not discussed royal commissions and task forces created by the provinces the trend toward special studies by social scientists as a standard part of the inquiry process is evident at this level as well. In particular, governments in Quebec have had frequent recourse to these informatiom-gathering instruments.
14 Carol Weiss, *Using Social Research in Public Policy-Making* (Lexington, Mass.: D.C. Heath 1977), 16.
15 See Meyer Bucovetsky, "The Mining Industry and the Great Tax Reform Debate," in *Pressure Group Behavior in Canadian Politics*, ed. Paul Pross (Toronto: McGraw-Hill Ryerson 1975), 87-114.
16 Richard Harris, *Trade, Industrial Policy and International Competition* (Toronto: University of Toronto Press 1985).
17 R. Simeon, ed., *Must Canada Fail?* (Montreal: McGill-Queen's University Press 1977), viii.
18 Ryan was the editor of the influential Quebec newspaper *Le Devoir*, before becoming leader of the Quebec Liberal Party in 1977.
19 D. Smiley, *Canada in Question: Federalism in the Eighties* (Toronto: McGraw-Hill Ryerson 1980), 261.

20 See David Kwavnick, "Quebec and the Two Nations Theory: a Re-examination," *Queen's Quarterly* 81, no. 3 (Autumn, 1974): 357-76.

21 Illustrations of these economic conditions are provided in J. Calvert, *Government Limited* (Ottawa: Canadian Centre for Policy Alternatives 1984), ch. 1; and D. Drache and D. Cameron, eds., *The Other Macdonald Report* (Toronto: Lorimer 1985), xiv, table I-1.

22 Drache and Cameron, *The Other Macdonald Report*, xiii.

23 See Richard Simeon, "Inside the Macdonald Commission," *Studies in Political Economy* 22 (Spring 1987): 167-79.

24 See G. Baum and D. Cameron, *Ethics and Economics: Canada's Catholic Bishops on the Economic Crisis* (Toronto: Lorimer 1984).

25 See the submission of the United Church's Working Unit on Social Issues and Justice to the Macdonald Commission. Parts of this document appear as "Economic Development and Social Justice," in Drache and Cameron, *The Other Macdonald Report*, 169-83.

26 Ibid., ix.

CHAPTER SEVEN

1 See the contributions by Janine Brodie and Jane Jenson, Neil Bradford, and Duncan Cameron on the question of the "language of politics" in *Canadian Parties in Transition: Discourse, Organization and Representation*, ed. A.G. Gagnon and A.B. Tanguay (Toronto: Nelson, 1988). These chapters examine the role of political parties in defining the content of political discourse.

2 There are of course exceptions to this generalization. See Lester Thurow, *Dangerous Currents: The State of Economics* (New York: Random House 1983).

3 In a recent survey of the development of the social sciences in Canada, John Trent observes that one of the most important issues during the last twenty-five years has been the influence of foreign personnel and theoretical approaches, contributing to a nationalist reaction in the social sciences. See "The Social Sciences in Canada in the Eighties," in *Global Crises and the Social Sciences: North American Perspectives*, ed. J. Trent and P. Lamy (Ottawa: University of Ottawa Press/UNESCO 1984), 53-5.

4 F.R. Scott, "W.L.M.K.," in *The Blasted Pine*, ed. F.R. Scott and A.J.M. Smith, rev. ed. (Toronto: Macmillan 1967), 36-7.

5 Alain G. Gagnon, "L'Influence de l'Eglise sur l'évolution socio-économique du Québec, de 1850 1950," *L'Action Nationale* 49, no. 4 (1979): 252-77.

6 Raymond Aron, *The Opium of the Intellectuals* (New York: W.W. Norton and Co. 1962), 217.

7 Samuel N. Eisenstadt, "Intellectuals and Political Elites," in *Intellectuals in Liberal Democracies*, ed. Alain G. Gagnon (New York: Praeger 1987), 157-65.

INDEX